# Becoming Hulda's Girls

Cover photo: Hulda E. Greenberg, c. 1930

## OUR READERS SPEAK OUT

"What a gift your book is! There's a bit of sorrow in finishing this book that I loved living within."

"Rather than telling a single story in chronilogical order - and thereby leaving out as much as they include - the authors have found a new and perfect form to convey the felt life of their very American childhood. This is a marvelous memoir!"

"I love your book. Can't put it down. It's warm and loving and honest. The details make it authentic. The Gotch girls have done it again!"

"I LOVE your book! The stories are so heart-warming and true for us Midwesterners."

"Your writing is like a creek flowing through different landscapes."

"I just finished your book; now I'm going to read it all over again. It's the best book I've read in years."

"I grew up near Boston, so how could my childhood have been so similar? But it was. I related to it all the way through."

"It is an impressive work, and a fitting tribute to Hulda. It makes clear what a wonderful mother she was as well as being a dedicated teacher."

"Such priceless photos, and I love the illustrations!"

# Becoming Hulda's Girls

## A Diary Memoir

Celebrating the Richness
of Everyday Life

## September to September

*Sharon Gotch Cobb*

Sharon Gotch Cobb
Linda Gotch Helmich
Marcia Gotch Micklos

Illustrations and Cover Design by
Linda Gotch Helmich

Barnhouse Books
Glenwood Springs, Colorado

Becoming Hulda's Girls
A Diary Memoir
Celebrating the Richness of Everyday Life
September to September

**Barnhouse Books**
4006 C.R. 115
Glenwood Springs CO   81601

ISBN: 978-0-615-99647-9
LCCN: 2014936583

1.AUTOBIOGRAPHY: Memoir
2.HISTORY/US/Midwest

First printing Aug. 2014, Second printing Nov. 2014

Printed in the United States of America

Dedicated to:
Mom and Dad
and
Marilyn

# CONTENTS

January brings an awareness of the richness
of living in close quarters and of being close.

February brings an awareness of the richness
of love in all its various forms.

March brings the richness of valuing what
every day has to offer.

April brings the richness of celebrating Easter
and the joy of new beginnings.

May brings an awareness of the richness of
having a mother who demonstrated the value of
caring for family, self, and others.

June brings the richness of the value of

entertaining ourselves and others, and the luxury of having *all the time in the world.*

In July, we experience the richness of travel and enjoying extended family.

August makes us realize the richness of the repeated rhythms that bring us back to where we were before, over and over again.

# Preface

Because we sisters are still wondering what we may become, and because we wish to understand who we are and how we got that way, we set out on a journey to discover who we were. Glancing back, and then digging in, we tasted the richness and as well as the bitterness of life that was part of our daily fare. We searched for clues that might reveal how it is that we Gotch girls, different from each other in so many ways, have kept and expressed a strong family loyalty and unity. Our search brought us to the realization that it had something to do with carrying on tradition, and living up to expectations. It also had a great deal to do with being nurtured by our wise and loving mother. As Marilyn wrote once in a note about her, "Her love and guidance will always be with us for we will draw strength from the valuable lessons of life that she lovingly taught us – love, friendship, compassion, faith, courage, (bearing) sorrow, and giving of oneself unselfishly." Her lessons of life gave us riches untold. Even though we were not materially rich, we were about as happy as anyone could be. We never had money, but we certainly were never poor. Shirley Temple Black once said, "Wealth wears many disguises." We agree.

*Riches*
*You are richer today than you were yesterday*
*if you have laughed often, given something, forgiven*
*even more, made a new friend today, or made step-*
*ping-stones of stumbling blocks.*

*You are richer if you have thought more in terms of*
*"Thyself" than "myself" or if you have managed to be*
*cheerful even if you were weary.*

*You are richer if a little child has smiled at you, or a*
*stray dog has licked your hand, or if you have looked*
*for the best in others, and given others the best in you.*

Author Unknown

In a diary/journal format, this memoir covers moments in time that happened over the course of a year, during the years 1938-1958. Some entries were things that happened once, others happened every year, and most were things that could have happened any year. They happened to one or the other of us or to all of us. The stories are true, or mostly true, as true as any memories can be. Taken as a whole, they show what our years were like, September to September.

You may want to read this book cover to cover, the conventional way to read a book, but you may choose to start with the month you are in now, and compare your month with ours, writing your impressions and insights at the end of each month. For fun, we have included various genre in the book, so you could focus in on the following features:

Poetry - April

Personality traits - January and Appendix E
Travel - July and August
Family folklore and history - Appendix A
Old recipes - Appendix B
Childhood games - Appendixes C and D

It is completely natural that we have written this book. As Vi Gura, our mother's friend from eighty years ago, said when she heard we were writing it, "Why, that's just what Hulda's girls would do." Did that make it easy? Absolutely not, but

*Where there's a will there's a way!*

We have enjoyed the process of finding out who we were. If we still aren't sure who we are, at least we know who we are becoming. We're Becoming Hulda's Girls!

If you have even half the fun reading this book that we have had writing it, it will have been worth the effort.

Keep becoming all you can be...

Marcia,                    (Marilyn),

*Marcia*                   *Marilyn*

Sharon,                    Linda

*Sharon*                   *Linda*

# WARNING:

This book was written by the girls that live inside of us - girls who talk about things you shouldn't really talk about or wouldn't if you were grown-up enough to know better, or things that should not be talked about outside of your diary, but then this *is* our diary, so please don't be offended or shocked or horrified. After all, these girls are still "becoming" and there is beauty in becoming, especially if you are...

"Becoming Hulda's Girls!"

Top: Marcia, Marilyn        Bottom: Sharon, Linda

# Chapter One        Any September
## *"There Goes Gotch..."*

**SEPT. 1**

*"There Goes Gotch..."* is painted on the back of the truck passing by. But what or who is a "Gotch?" Gotch is the name of the family that owns the truck, the same family that owns Gotch Radio Specialties, a local appliance and record store located in the small Midwestern town of Streator, Illinois, the same family that produced the Gotch Girls, as we are known in our community, four sisters, us. "Which one are you?" people ask. "Are you one of the twins?" (Marcia and Marilyn) "or the redhead?" (Sharon) "or the baby?" (Linda)

**SEPT. 2**

We live our lives from September to September. Our mother is a schoolteacher, so our lives revolve around the school calendar. To get off to a good start, to put our best foot forward, we always begin the year with a new dress, just as Mom has always done. Dresses are for good and for school. Pants are for play.

*Always put your best foot forward. You only get one chance to make a good first impression.*

[Note: Our mother, Hulda Emma (Greenberg) Gotch, taught thirty-two years for the Streator public school system. Almost all of those years, she taught fourth grade.] Throughout this book, all notes in brackets are historical comments.

### SEPT. 3

The first day of school is our New Year's Day. Every year we look forward to this special event with great anticipation. In our new school dresses and shoes, with our hair done just right, with our new school supplies in tow, and with butterflies in our stomachs, we practically fly to school, eager to see what the new year will bring. Even though we know most of our new teachers personally, since they are Mom's friends, it doesn't stop us from feeling thrilled. In fact, it makes us feel very special. Hannah becomes Mrs.Kief, Betty becomes Mrs. Spirduso, Frieda becomes Miss Hoyle, etc., and Mom becomes Mrs. Gotch, even to us, at least when we are at school.

### SEPT. 4

When we aren't in school and we're not at home, we are usually at our store, the Gotch Radio. Our father, Frank, and his two brothers own the store, but Dad runs it, doing all of the buying, selling, and book-keeping, opening it every morning, locking it up every night, year after year. It's really his business, and our business.

In the front of the store, he sells refrigerators, sinks

and stoves; behind that, are the console phonographs and televisions. In the middle of the store, across from the office, are the irons, toasters, radios, and transistor radios. In the back of the store, is the record department, where Aunt Millie and we girls, sell records of all kinds, 33 1/3 albums, stacked row after row in bins, 45 rpm singles, kept on the counter, and occasionally an old 78 rpm, which line the wall behind the counter. Hidden away, in the very back of the building, Uncle Johnny fixes radios and TV's in the repair shop. Listening to classical music, he tests tubes with their glowing squiggles of light inside, and using a soldering iron, he fiddles with electronic gadgets he pulls from countless little drawers that line the wall.

We swing on the Dutch door that separates his area from the walkway, and play in the zoo-like cage that houses the radios that were fixed long ago, but are now forgotten. Last but not least, for the convenience of the farmers who buy our gas stoves, we have a large metal container out in the alley behind the store, full of propane gas tanks, so heavy only Dad can pick them up. This very likely makes us the store with the greatest number of "specialties" on all of Main Street.

### SEPT. 5

Aunt Millie never tires of teaching us good business practices like making change by counting it back with all the bills facing one direction, thanking the customer with eye contact and a smile, knowing our inventory, and following the Golden Rule for problem situations: "The customer is always right." On these and all other matters of life and love, Aunt Millie always knows, or thinks she knows, the right way. Most of the time we agree.

*The customer is always right.*

[However, Aunt Millie's opinion that rock 'n' roll was too inferior to have a lasting impact on the world certainly did not prove to be true.]

## SEPT. 6

Having a father who runs a record shop is ideal for us Gotch girls. Dad very generously lets us have any record we ask for, resulting in our having a very large collection even though we try not to abuse his generosity too terribly. He may spoil us a little bit, but we are not paid for most of the hours we work at the store, which is every day after school until five-thirty when we are in high school, Friday nights until we close at nine, and sometimes all day Saturday, in addition to every nine a.m. to nine p.m. day of the two weeks before Christmas. That is a lot of unpaid work hours! At times, it is unclear why we are popular. Is it because we are who we are, or is it because we own the best record collection in town? Nobody knows.

## SEPT. 7

Our home, a cozy little two bedroom house, is perfectly located on the corner, four blocks south of town, two blocks east of church, and two blocks west of school. Mom and Dad share one bedroom. We girls, all four of us, share the other, one older and one younger girl in each bed. Other rooms include a living room with a dining area, a kitchen with a breakfast nook, our favorite place to congregate, and one small bathroom with a tub. Home sweet home.

*No matter how humble, there's no place like home.*

Because we sell them at the store, our Youngstown kitchen is the latest thing, with white metal built-in cabinets, a sink that has porcelain drain boards on each side, and even a spray nozzle. In one corner of the kitchen is a handy clothes chute for dropping dirty clothes right to the basement where they land near the washing machine. On top of the clothes chute is our rotary dial telephone. If you want to give us a buzz, our phone number is 50361.

Our neighbors on either side, the one to the south and the one to the west, have the same exact floor plan that we have, but we have the biggest yard because we are on the corner. Mom says that is just one more reason to be thankful. She's right; we love having a nice big yard to play in.

*Always remember to count your blessings.*

## SEPT. 8

We never lose track of time or our spiritual lives with St. Anthony's, our Roman Catholic Church, just two blocks away. It's Westminster chimes ring from the steeple every fifteen minutes, twenty-four hours a day. We are so used to them that we hardly hear them unless we wonder what time it is. Then we listen, and pretty soon the chimes tell us. At midnight, they ring twelve loud gongs, but we never even hear them since we are sound asleep.

There are five Catholic churches in our small, rural town and some other Protestant churches which we know nothing about, since we are forbidden to go to Protestant churches. Our mother was raised a

Protestant, but when she married Dad, becoming a Catholic, she vowed to give her children a Catholic upbringing, which is what she is doing. When we share what we learn from the nuns at Catechism, that Roman Catholics are the only ones who are saved, Mom always says that she doesn't believe that all of her godly Protestant relatives are lost. That is her simple statement, and nothing more. We hope she is right, and the nuns are wrong, because we love those relatives.

SEPT. 9

Every Sunday we swarm to church with most of our neighbors for blocks around, dressed fit to kill with gloves and purses, missals, and hats.* The service lasts about forty-five minutes, and when we come home, the aroma of Sunday roast with potatoes and carrots is waiting for us. On Sundays, we eat in the dining room, setting the table with a nice tablecloth, using cloth napkins and the real silver silverware , saying grace, and using our best manners.

[The heads of all women and girls had to be covered. If a hat or scarf could not be found, we could bobby pin a hanky or tissue on our head, but that looked really stupid, so we rarely did it. Men and boys, on the other hand, had to always remove their hats in church, as a sign of respect.]

SEPT. 10

Later, on Sundays, we sometimes visit Grandma Gotch, who lives just four houses down from us in a beautiful gray Victorian we call "the Big House". Dad was born and raised in this house. He rode his tricycle

on the sidewalk, the same sidewalk we use, only now
it's cracked and broken in some places. He attended
the same grade school we now attend (Plumb), and his
high school (SHS) will some day be our alma mater as
well.

Grandma gives us lemon drops she keeps in
her apron pocket, and fixes us root beer floats. The
twins and Sharry love to go down to spend time
with Grandma, especially fun on a hot day when the
iceman delivers ice for the icebox that sits on the back
porch, as he will always chip off a chunk that you
can suck on, letting it drip all down your chest and
tummy, cooling you off.

[Eventually the icebox was replaced with a Philco
refrigerator from our store. Grandma Gotch died when
Linda was only three.]

SEPT. 11

We celebrate every holiday at the Big House,
carrying out our family traditions, each holiday
bringing its own special rituals, but some of them
remaining the same. Every Thanksgiving, Christmas
and Easter, Uncle Johnny buys a case of Pepsi, and a
case of 7up for us to enjoy. Other than an occasional
trip to the root beer stand, holidays are the only time
we are allowed to drink pop, but on those days, we
can have as much as we want. Aunt Millie brings
the ham or turkey, Aunt Tillie bakes the pies, Aunt
Marie brings the heavenly fruit salad and the relish
tray, and Mom makes the vegetable casseroles. All
of the uncles bring their appetites and thirst for a
little holiday cheer. No holiday is complete without an
abundant supply of rushka, our traditional Slovakian

sweet bread with the walnut, apricot or poppy seed filling*.

*See appendix B for recipe.

## SEPT. 12

Monday through Friday, we walk to our neighborhood school, Ralph Plumb School, which we call "Plumb" for short. Plumb is the three-story red brick block of a building where we have all started in the kindergarten on the first floor, worked our way up to the second floor which holds grades one through four around a fairly large central landing, on up to the top floor which has the last four grades with the hall in the middle, just like the middle floor. The room on the left as you get to the landing of the second floor is our mother's fourth grade classroom, which, just walking past, gives us a special feeling of pride and joy.

The magnificent staircase, made of thick, solid golden oak, its banisters silky smooth, and stair treads nicely worn on both the up and down sides, the staircase that greets us warmly as we first enter the building, speaks to us that we are a part of a long and rich tradition of learning. Halfway up the stairs to the top floor, in the front of the building, is the principal's office. We are thrilled if we are sent on a special errand to the office, but we never want to be sent there to be disciplined, of course. Boys are unruly enough to get the paddle sometimes, but that would never happen to us girls who love to do whatever our teachers ask us to do because we adore our teachers.

At the back of the school, in the same position as the office, is the teacher's bathroom. It has a little cot in it where you may lie down if you are not feeling well, or if you have cramps because it's that time of the month. Each of the classrooms has a cloakroom next to it, a long narrow hallway with a row of black metal hooks for our coats and scarves, and our galoshes and wet wool mittens puddling water on the floor, a cloakroom where most of the best secrets are shared. Across the hall from the kindergarten, on the right, is the gymnasium, with wire mesh on the windows. We play Dodge ball in there if it is raining or is too snowy outside.

In the back on the bottom floor are the bathrooms, boys' on the left, girls' on the right. By the boys' bathroom is the big furnace that the janitor, Andy Yuhas, takes care of, even as he takes care of us. He is a kindly, gentle man, with a warm smile, who knows all of our names, knows all of our brothers and sisters, and knows how to find whatever we have lost.

Between the furnace in back and the kindergarten room in the front is the v-shaped cloakroom of the kindergarten. That is where we all go when we have a drill for an atomic bomb because it has no windows, making it the safest place. For tornado drills, we just crawl under our desks, and get away from the windows. For fire drills, we go outside. If we are upstairs, we have to walk down the metal fire escape on the outside of the building, a pretty scary excursion because you can see through the grates all the way to the ground, giving you the feeling you could fall, even though you are perfectly safe.

**SEPT. 13**

Like most of the other students, we live in town, but a few of the students live out in the country. They are the only ones who ride a bus to school. They have to bring their brown paper bag lunches, with their sandwiches wrapped in wax paper, leaving them in the cloakroom until lunchtime. If anyone brings tuna fish salad, it smells up the whole cloakroom! We are happy to be able to skip, walk, or run home for lunch. We usually have grilled cheese, peanut butter or bologna sandwiches and the new canned tomato or chicken noodle soup. It has to be something Mom can whip up fast, because we all have to get back to school.

Seeing the country kids and a number of other friends who don't live in our immediate neighborhood is part of the fun of getting back to school. We miss them over the summer, and are glad to be back together again. Some years, though not very often, a new student will be added to our classes, and that is always interesting, as usually it is just the same kids, year after year.

*It feels so good to get back to the old routines.*
*There's nothing like routine!*

**SEPT. 14**

Like Dad, the twins completed all eight years at Plumb, but Sharon and Linda have been able to go to Oakland Park School (OPS), the new K-12 school they built that includes a junior high school, grades seven and eight. All of the seventh and eighth graders south of Main Street now go to this junior high. If you live north of Main Street, and are in junior high, you go to Northlawn. Mom transferred from Plumb, too, and is teaching fourth grade in the wing for lower grades.

This school has an exciting new wrinkle, a hot lunch program. How we love that homemade chili and apple crisp, the best we've ever had! Amazing new courses are offered, like Home Economics for the girls, where we are learning to cook and sew, and for the boys, Shop class, where they are learning to use tools.

The most shocking experience of all was when we had to take group showers after physical education (P.E.). This was the first shower we ever had since we only have a tub at home. Some of us have bodies that are growing and changing and some do not. Either way, it's really embarrassing.

**SEPT. 15**

There is nothing like going to a brand new school with not a scratch on anything. No graffiti on the walls or bathroom stalls! Shiny clean waxed floors! No squeaky doors! It's the best. Sharon was fortunate enough to be in the very first graduating class, but Linda is not far behind. A stellar student, Sharon received many honors in junior high school, but her final encore balanced them out. She was graciously invited to turn the piano player's pages at the graduation ceremony in lieu of participating in the chorus consisting of all of the other students. What an honor. One can only imagine the conversation of those in power trying to decide what to do with the tone-deaf student who happened to be the daughter of a fellow teacher and friend. Linda, attending junior high a couple of years later, has surprised the music teacher by being able to sing quite well.

**SEPT. 16**

Since it's the middle of September, we are all pretty well oriented to our new classrooms. Things seem to be running smoothly. Marcia is struggling, as she often does, over difficult homework, struggling with the unfairness that she has to work so much harder than Marilyn to get the same amount of work done. "You are all very different," Mom reminds us. "Just do what needs to be done, and do your best. That's all I expect of you." "Even C's are average," she says, but we know she wants us to get something better than "average".

*Just do what needs to be done, and do your best.*

SEPT. 17

In my (Linda's) third grade class, the most amazing things happened. For one thing, when we arrived, all of the brown desks had been painted pink and blue, yellow and green. On top of that, instead of being in straight rows, the way it has always been, the teacher had the desks placed in little groups. These ideas are so totally new! We think it is quite fun!

We are taking turns being the teacher for a day, too. It feels so important to be the teacher! We have decorated the room to look like a circus, and we are going to do a performance where we show how we have learned to do backward and forward somersaults and a few other tricks. I sure hope Mom or Dad can come. They are going to try to catch at least part of the show.

[Linda kept one eye on the door throughout the afternoon, but neither one came. Most of the mothers were there, since hardly any of them worked outside the home, and even some dads were there. Sometimes it was hard to have working parents.]

**SEPT. 18**

September is birthday month at our house. Three out of four of us have our birthdays this month. Sharon's is the nineteenth, and the twins' is the twentieth. It is a good time for Linda, too, because presents can't be given to all three of the other girls and leave her out, so she always is given a little something as well. Mom and her helper, Linda, are busy baking today, the day before. Sharon always wants chocolate cake, so that's what she gets. She loves being the prima donna on her birthday (or any other day for that matter).

**SEPT. 19**

Birthdays are always special but not extravagant. This is the one truly extravagant one for Sharry. Aunt Martha and Uncle Clarence have surprised her with a brand spanking new green and silver chrome Schwinn bicycle, "the top of the line," Mom says. Sharry is ecstatic, but Marcia and Marilyn are rather sad. They have wanted bicycles for a long time, but Mom and Dad said they were too dangerous, so they weren't allowed to have one. Linda is excited because she thinks this means maybe she will get one, too, someday.

[And one day she did. She and Dad went together, just the two of them, up to Van Loon's, to get a bicycle. She picked out a smaller, nice blue Schwinn with training wheels, not so flashy, not top of the line, but perfect for her. How exciting! To this day, the smell of tires, like the smell of Van Loon's, makes her heart skip a beat. These bicycles had no gears; the speed you went was determined by how fast you pedaled. The brakes functioned by pressing down on the back pedal, and they always had a kick stand so you could park your bike anywhere. We never locked up our bikes, and they were never stolen. Sadly, the twins never did get bicycles.]

## SEPT. 20 THE TWINS' BIRTHDAY

[Marcia and Marilyn's extra special birthday was their eighteenth, when they were freshmen at Illinois State Normal University. Aunt Martha and Uncle Clarence gave them a party at their beautiful home in Bloomington. Grandpa Greeneberg, in his nineties, was able to come, which was neat because we rarely saw him. Aunt Martha used her finest linens, dishes, and manners to create an elegant affair, never to be forgotten.]

## SEPT. 21

The day after all those birthdays is always a pretty big letdown, so you just have to make the best of it. Thank goodness for school. There are spelling words to be memorized, multiplication tables to be learned, books to be read, book reports to be written, penmanship to be practiced, and art projects to be created using the colorful leaves that have begun to fall.

## SEPT. 22

We are really fortunate to grow up in the world of Make Believe. Mom values our imaginations and frequently encourages us to use them. We seldom are bored, but if we are, Mom makes this simple suggestion: "Put on your little thinking caps; you'll think of something." And we do.

Our basement is a treasure-trove of possibilities, storing the leftovers from Mom's teaching buffet, a varied menu of tag board stencils, fragrant purple ditto sheets, construction paper fragments, and workbooks galore, generally speaking at the fourth grade level. If you are in fifth grade they are pretty easy, but if you are in third grade, a bit of a challenge, perfect for playing school, which we do, hour after hour after hour.

## SEPT. 23

After school, Mom says children should go outside to play in the fresh air and sunshine; six hours is long enough to be cooped up inside. That is why she never assigns homework to her students. We like that idea.

*All work and no play makes Jack a dull boy.*

Having completed a busy day teaching school, Mom puts the dinner on to cook and stretches out on the couch to read the Streator Daily Times Press which is delivered to our door by the neighborhood paper boy at about five o'clock. Before long, she dozes off for a few minutes with the paper over her face. That is her quiet space. We know she needs this little rest, so if we come in, we quietly tiptoe around her.

Otherwise she uses every minute productively. She does her manicures in the car, practices cursive while waiting in the doctor's office, and remembers everyone's birthday and every appointment she has recorded in her little date book which she always carries in her purse.

## SEPT. 24

September's calendar, which hangs above the telephone, always displays a beautiful New England countryside in autumn. You can see a covered bridge, a charming white church, and beautiful hills of color. It looks like a place we'd like to visit someday.

[Sharon has lived in New England most of her adult life.]

## SEPT. 25

Sharon is in Mom's class when she is in fourth grade. Having your own mother for a teacher presents some unique challenges. Here are a few:

-Some kids think Mom and I sleep at school because we always seem to be there when they arrive and when they leave. We don't. I tell them we don't, but they won't believe me.

-Some kids say she can't be my mother because she's my teacher. I try to explain how she is both. "You just call her 'Mom' because you like her," they say.

-Sometimes I need a mom at home to confide in instead of a mom who is my teacher. I want to complain about how stupid the math homework is, but there is no compassionate mom to listen to my complaint. She just says, "Never mind complaining. Buckle down and get to work; you'll be done before you know it."

-It's strange not being able to share what happened at school, like other children do. What good would it do? Mom already knows what happened at school.

## SEPT. 26

Some things we keep secret from the kids at school:

- Mom always takes off her good teaching dress when she gets home from school, and then, sometimes, especially on warm days, she is around the house just in her slip. I never tell that to the class. She has never told me not to; I just know.

- Mom also likes a sip of beer now and then on a hot day, or on a holiday. I never mention this in class, either.

[In those days drinking alcohol, even being seen in a bar, was considered grounds for losing your job as a teacher because drinking was considered a sign of moral weakness. Teachers were held to the very highest moral and ethical standards since they served as models for the children.]

- To Mom's chagrin, Dad has too may beers at times, ending up being pretty tipsy. Then Mom says he is "three sheets to the wind." He always disagrees, protesting that he is fine. No need to mention this sort of thing in class. I know better than that!

*You don't have to say every thought*
*that comes into your head.*

SEPT. 27

What's in a name? Here is how it works when Sharon is in Mom's class. If they are getting along well at home, which isn't too often, Sharon calls her "Mom" in class, and Mom smiles and responds by calling her "Sharry". When things are not going so well at home, Sharon calls her "Mrs. Gotch", and Mom addresses

her as "Sharon". In general, her name is "Sharon" at
school, and "Sharry" at home. Do you suppose any of
the other students ever notice?

SEPT. 28

Mom wants to make sure that she doesn't give
special treatment to Sharon while they are in class.
She knows favoritism can lead to hard feelings on the
part of the other children, so if Sharry needs extra
help with something, which happens occasionally,
Mom quietly reminds her, " I can do this with you at
home." It works.

SEPT. 29

"Marcia, Marilyn, Sharon and Linda," exactly in
our birth order, is the way Mom calls us whenever she
wants us all to come. Sometimes she might just want
Linda, but ends up going through the whole list until
she gets to the one she wants. "Marc, Mar, Shar...
Linda," she says.

Also, at home, if we are in trouble, Mom will often
address us by our full names, all four of them. That's
how we know she means business. We all have four
names, the third one being our confirmation name.
Here are our full names: Marcia Marie Martha Gotch,
Marilyn Lou Mary Gotch, Sharon Ann Marie Gotch,
and Linda Lee Anne Gotch

SEPT. 30

Sharon ponders her choice to be an educator, following in Mom's footsteps: I owe my whole teaching career
to having had Mrs. Gotch (Mom) for my fourth grade
teacher. In order to keep this high-energy daughter
usefully occupied, and out of trouble, Mom gave me

assistant teaching-type jobs on a daily basis, including giving the slowest reading group, the ones who had not yet found joy in reading, some extra coaching.

"I think you are just the one to get those yellow birds going," Mom encouraged. "You've got what it takes, and I'll show you how."

That seed that was planted, that taste of the joy that comes in passing on knowledge, know-how, and the pleasure of learning was all it took. Though there were temptations to enter fields offering more fame and fortune, they could never compete, for the passion that started in fourth grade was not to be denied. A satisfying career of over thirty-five years in education was the end result.

[Marilyn spent most of her life in education as well. Marcia, who studied to be a teacher in college, used what she had learned in raising a large family. Linda was the one who broke the mold by becoming a nurse, and later an artist and writer. Marilyn and Sharon liked to write, as well.]

SEPT. 31

Mrs. Gotch is well known and liked in our community. When we go to town, we often run into people who say they have had our mother for fourth grade, and that she is their all-time favorite teacher. It's surprising because sometimes they look older than she does. You teach many, many people in thirty-two years! She's popular, but she's strict, too. Without raising her voice, without being angry, she keeps things under control, usually allowing no monkey business, no shenanigans. Without saying anything, she commands our respect. Most of the time we do

what she asks, as do her students, just because we love
her so.

[How did her girls ever turn out so playful? "What
will you think of next?" she used to ask.]

# Memories of My School Years

Frank, Open for
business.

GOTCH RADIO SPECIALTIES
123 SOUTH MONROE STREET
STREATOR, ILLINOIS

Millie & Johnnie @ the Shop

FRANK R. GOTCH

TELEPHONE 34024

The

Gotch

Radio

Linnie in the repair shop

Ralph Plumb School

Frankie, six yrs. old

St. Anthony's

Miss

Greenberg

Nipper, the RCA
Victor dog

The Gotch Family
on the front porch

The twins with Grandma Gotch

The Clothes Chute

The twins with Grandpa
Greeneberg, 18th B-day

Sharry & Linda w/ S's new
bike and Friskie

# Chapter Two        Any October
## *Mysterious Happenings*

**OCT. 1**

*Leaves flutter by.*
*Chills creep in.*
*Days fleet by.*
*Fall has arrived.*

**OCT. 2**

Jack Frost came last night, and in a most magical way, looking really hand painted, all of the leaves have begun to turn, sugar maples shockingly red, oaks orangey-brown, elms a nice warm gold. Later on, after all the leaves have fallen, and before the snow arrives, we will have a time when everything is just brown, a rather sad grayish-brown, sad and yet beautiful in a way, like train whistles in the distance are sad and beautiful at the same time.

[Streator had five major railroads going through the

town, so one could almost always hear a train whistle in the distance. Now, for us, train whistles sound like "home". When we lived there, they always sounded like a call to go somewhere else.]

*There's a nip in the air; it must be fall.*

OCT. 3

Walking is a constant part of our lives. We walk to church, walk to school, walk to town, walk to the park to play on the swings, walk to dance and piano lessons; we even walk the long twelve blocks to and from high school. Walking to town in the fall is especially delightful, shuffling our feet through the leaves, kicking up little clouds of leaf fragrance, rustling our way block after block. How fortunate we are to have big elm trees lining both sides of our street.

[Many of these beautiful trees died of the Dutch elm disease in the late 1950's.]

OCT. 4

Sharon loves dancing with the leaves. Falling leaves churn up her spirit, calling her to join them. She dances ever so lightly, but briskly among them, twirling in the wind, becoming a part of their beautiful descent to earth, her flaming red hair swirling with the vibrant ribbons of red, orange, yellow, and brown, flowing down and around, down and around, down to the ground, spent.

*The best things in life are free.*

**OCT. 5**

The recent frosts have reminded us, not happily
so, that winter is right around the corner with its
wind and snow and ice, but then we are pleasantly
surprised by the *Chicago Sunday "Trib"*, with its
*Injun Summer* painting on the front, heralding the
return of warm weather for a bit, a very welcome bit.
Indian Summer, those warm, golden halcyon days,
days we will drink in and try to hold onto as long as
possible, storing up that sunny feeling, so that, in the
days ahead, when the gray of winter is upon us, we
may close our eyes and feel it once again.

**OCT. 6**

The wind has really been blowing lately, so we have
had to wear our babushkas whenever we are outside,
but it has been great for bringing down the leaves.
Our dictionary tells how much we all love beautiful
fall leaves. Whenever you open it to look up a word,
flattened treasures fall out, carefully pressed leaves,
placed there in preparation for some future project
that is long forgotten by the time the leaves are dry.
Some of these little surprises seem to be from previous
years judging from how very brittle and fragile they
are, while others are still a bit moist, the ones we just
put in last week perhaps, ones we picked up on the
way home from school, too lovely to pass by.

**OCT. 7**

We love leaf projects, so it is good to have a ready
supply. One of our favorites is to do simple rubbings,
placing a piece of paper over the lines, curves and
veins of the leaf and rubbing a crayon over it. By doing
this, you can see how exquisitely they are made.

Another project is using a warm iron to press the leaves between sheets of wax paper, the wax melting slightly, holding the leaves in place, especially nice when using tiny leaves to make bookmarks. It's fun making these decorations, but we don't really have walls that can be decorated since our bedroom walls are too rough for tape to stick to them, so they become gifts for Mom. She will, no doubt, end up storing them in the old buffet in the basement, which is full of such treasures.

[People did not use refrigerators to display artwork in those days.]

OCT. 8

The most exciting project, an all day affair, is building a leaf house, a floor plan of leaves that covers the whole side yard. The process starts with running and chasing each other, tossing about the leaves. When this phase is no longer fun, we all work together to rake the leaves into tall piles, hard work for little arms using big rakes with missing tines. Once the piles have been assembled, we take turns taking flying leaps into the leaves, similar to a belly flop dive into a lake, always accompanied by shrieks of delight, the bigger the flop, the louder the wail. Eventually that, too, loses its glamour. The next step is to rake again, clearing the area to make room for the walls, doorways, and window openings. The twins do most of the wall building, with Sharon following behind picking up the dropped leaves. Linda goes into the house to drag out toys and dolls that will be used to play "house" in our fine new leaf house.

[Dad taught this activity to Marcia and Marilyn when they were little. They passed it on to Sharon and Linda. Do you suppose, in making such large homes with many rooms, we were sort of wishing or dreaming that we could live in a house with all that space? Maybe.]

*Many hands make light work.*

### OCT. 9

Friskie, our kitten, loves to play in the leaves. He seems to think each leaf is a mouse waiting to be pursued; any sudden rustle makes him pounce, making us chuckle at his funny antics. Scampering back and forth between the rooms of our leaf house, causing the leaf walls to tumble down, he shows no concern for all of the work we have put into them.

### OCT. 10

The most tedious fall job we undertake is making our acorn pipes, digging out the inside of the acorn with much difficulty, since, being girls, we don't just have our own pocketknives we can use. For that reason, we are forced to use less efficient tools, like bobby pins, hairpins, a small screwdriver, or, heaven forbid, the old ice pick, which we ferret out of the junk drawer in the kitchen. Big sisters, indeed, have to help little sisters.

Why we want to make pipes is a mystery. The only person we know who smokes a pipe is Frosty the Snowman, but we never save our pipes for him. For whatever reason, or, perhaps, for no reason at all, we like to make them. Of course we never really smoke them. They are just pretend. After removing the cap and digging out the inside, we poke a hole in the side and insert a stick for the stem of the pipe. Other times, acorns that fall from the tree out front are used as cups or pretend snacks for tea parties.

[As a grown-up, Sharon actually smoked a small pipe for a while. Maybe she was trying to go back to these happy days. Mom would occasionally mention that her father smoked a pipe with cherry tobacco in it when she was young, so she still enjoyed that smell. She never complained about the smoke from Dad's cigarettes.]

**OCT. 11**

By this time of the month, we are beginning to have conversations about what we want to *be* for Halloween. "What are you going to be?" we ask, wanting to know if the idea we have is already taken or still available. Some people don't like Halloween: the costumes, the jaunt into the night, the candy, all that spookiness, but we love it. It's like dressing up for one of Mom's plays that she directs at the community theatre, only better.

Linda is content to be a clown several years in a row, and enjoys being a bum with eyebrow pencil stubble, but she may try something different this year. Sharon's greatest challenge is to decide which one of her great ideas is the best, as she wants to have the most creative and unusual costume. Of course, the easy answer for her is to use one of her dance costumes. Marcia will go along with whatever idea Marilyn comes up with, and Marilyn will think of something for sure. Last year they were gypsies with colorful scarves and gold bangle bracelets. With nothing really decided, we keep pondering it all of the rest of the month.

## OCT. 12

One day this month we spend helping Mom prepare her classroom bulletin board for the annual Columbus Day celebration. Mom changes her bulletin board at least every month, and always takes great pride in making them interesting and fun, as well as instructive. We look forward to putting up the elaborate ships with all of their sails and rigging on a whole bulletin board full of ocean waves. The Nina, The Pinta, and The Santa Maria – we love the sound of those names. After a while, all those waves become tedious, taking so long to make that we feel we were the ones making the trip to America for the first time. What a voyage it must have been!

## OCT. 13

Since most of the leaves have fallen, it is finally, time to burn the leaves at the edge of the berm out front. This is a special time we share with Dad, for he knows how to keep the fire safely under control, just how many leaves to add to the pile each time. Still, we seem to be courting danger as we see the flames shoot up in the air as more leaves are added. It's exciting and fun. We love it, and we love to be doing something just with our Dad.

Fortunately, there are many leaves to rake and burn, all from that one big oak tree out front, a tree that isn't even ours, a tree that grows just over the boundary line, in the Ross' yard. "So many leaves to rake," Mom chuckles, "and not a tree in the yard!" That means the process continues hour after hour,

Dad patiently tending the fire, we coming and going, but returning to watch the last embers glowing red against the darkening evening light, mesmerized.

*Mmm... just smell those burning leaves!*

OCT. 14

We Gotch Girls love the smell of burning leaves! How could we describe that aroma? It's not a *bad* smell like fertilizer or horse manure or something rotten. It's not a *flowery* smell like perfume or talcum powder or soap, nor a *sweet* smell like apple pie or chocolate chip cookies or banana bread. But could the smell of burning leaves be about the same as the *taste* of roasted marshmallows?

OCT. 15

The taste of fall is a crunchy, creamy, salty, juicy, drippy, sticky caramel apple rolled in chopped peanuts from George's Candy Store. The only time it is possible to get these treats is for a couple of weeks just after the apples are picked. We check the display *daily* to see if they are in yet. One more day. One more day. At last they arrive. Oh, the taste of fall! Thank you, Johnny Appleseed!

[Check out the story of Johnny Appleseed on line sometime; it's a really neat story about a man who planted apple trees all over the new frontier, west of Massachusetts.]

## OCT. 16

Lately, we have had a real mystery to solve in our family. Uncle Johnny, noticing that spare parts from the repair shop were disappearing, began reporting the missing parts, day after day, to Dad. Dad thought Uncle Johnny was just forgetting which parts he had used, but Uncle Johnny was convinced that was not the case. They really were disappearing!

He wanted to solve the mystery and prove he was right, so, using his electronic skills, Uncle Johnny set up a secret camera to see who the culprit was. We had never heard of anything like that, but it worked! The hired deliveryman was sneaking in at night and stealing those parts. Caught red-handed by the camera, he had to go straight to jail! That is good, but what will happen when he gets out? What then? It's a scary thought.

[Fortunately, we never heard from him again.]

## OCT. 17

Halfway between our house and the Big House lives (horrors!) Old Lady Shively, our spooky neighbor. She lives alone in a shabby gray skeleton of a house that hasn't a shred of paint. Her screens are torn, her yard overgrown. She never goes anywhere, never talks to anyone, and seldom does anyone come to visit her. On rare occasions, a man in a black car drives up, enters, stays a short time, and leaves. How mysterious is that?

Occasionally, one of the balls we are playing with lands in her yard. Out of nowhere, she appears, grabs our ball, and disappears back into her house screaming in a high shrill voice, " You kids stay out

of my yard! You have no business being in my yard!"
We never see our ball again. Dad says she did the
same thing when he was a kid.

Once we saw her sitting out on her front stoop
combing her hair, whitish yellow and long, all the way
down to her waist, so like a *witch*. That was all we
needed to keep us away for good. We definitely never
go *there* to trick or treat!

[Of course, she was not a witch. She was just a
lonely old lady who did not want to be disturbed by
boisterous children. We still wonder what happened to
all of our balls, though.]

OCT. 18

Another scary thing that happened in our
neighborhood was a horrendous storm when lightning
struck the Laundromat behind Goluba's neighborhood
store, the store where we buy our penny candy and
occasional loaves of wonder bread. Only a block from
our house! What an explosion! What a burst of flames!
What sirens! Sharry has been a scaredy-cat about it
ever since. Her kindergarten teacher has tried to help
her get over being so afraid of the place by taking
the class by there every day during their outing.
On several occasions, though, Sharry has become
hysterical. Now, if they are going that way, they just
leave her behind in the principal's office. Some things
are just too scary to handle.

OCT. 19

Fires are always extremely frightening for us.

[Historical note: Once there was a fire in our town

that was so huge and so devastating it scared the
whole town. One morning, a few folks noted a slight
smell of gas as they opened up Williams Hardware,
the largest hardware store in town, but no one thought
too much about it. By ten o'clock in the morning,
when the store was full of customers, it suddenly blew
up, an explosion that could be felt for blocks around,
followed by a raging fire, for it was a huge three-story
building. Some people were blown right out the door,
and some who were walking by were blown across the
street. Six people lost their lives and many more were
injured. Our town was in mourning for a long, long
time. A smoky dark hole was on the site for years, and
they never rebuilt that three-story building. It haunts
us still.

This fire took place on July 14, 1958. Torrential
rain the night before may have caused flooding of the
coal mines below the store resulting in gas pockets
being formed, gas leaking into the store, and possible
ignition by a spark from the elevator. ]

**OCT. 20**

This evening started off normal enough. We were
sitting around the breakfast nook doing our homework
as usual, when we began to notice a faint smell of
smoke. We wondered if something was burning on the
stove or in the oven. No. We wondered if there was
an electrical problem in the basement. Mom checked
the gray metal fuse box by the washing machine.
Everything looked fine. Dad had gone to bed early,
but there was no need to wake him. The smell was
there, but not too strong. Maybe it was coming in
from outside. Maybe the neighbors were burning their
rubbish. No. Maybe an ashtray had been emptied

before the cigarette was completely out. Mom checked
the garbage can, but no.

The haze was increasing, as was Mom's blood
pressure, but we could find no source for the smoke.
Finally, Linda went to get something from the dark
front bedroom where Dad was sleeping, and there,
lo and behold, at the head of the bed, was a glowing
red circle. Dad had been sleeping right next to the
source of all that smoke and never even woke up!
Pandemonium broke out. The smoldering foam pillow,
set afire by Dad's cigarette, was quickly removed to
outside and drenched with water. Mystery solved.

[After that, Dad didn't smoke in bed anymore.]

**OCT. 21**

[Our store was part of a large building that
stretched nearly half a city block or more. In two
stories, next to the alley, it housed Rosalind Hupp's
dance studio on the top floor, where Sharry took her
lessons, and a financial place downstairs. Next to
that was the Granada movie theatre, then the Jewel
Beauty Shop, Dr. Williams' optical shop, Mulford
Printing, and one of those new pizza parlors, the S & W.

One night, Mom and Dad woke us up in the middle
of the night. They had gotten a call telling them that
there was a fire in the pizza kitchen, and now the
whole building was on fire. Even before we left home,
we could see the glow in the dark sky from the flames
below. After driving to the area, we were sickened
by the horrifying sight before us. The flames were
engulfing the far end of the building. Rosalind Hupp's
studio was already gone, the movie theatre, too. The
Jewel was gone, and the optical shop as well. Though

the firemen were valiantly struggling to save the building, the flames moved closer and closer to our store. We were trembling and in tears; all we could do was hug each other and pray. "Please, God, don't let it burn down our store!" Just as the flames reached our store, it stopped. The double firewall Dad had insisted be built years ago had done the job. There seemed to be smudges everywhere in the store from the smoke, and it took many weeks or months before the burny smell went away, but our end of the building and almost all of the merchandise had been saved.]

[This fire happened April 24, 1963. The happy row of stores was never replaced, and sadly ended up being just a parking lot.]


**OCT. 22**

The spirit of Halloween is in the air. Jack-o-lanterns are appearing everywhere. We Gotch girls usually make two large ones, one for each side of the porch. Eagerly we gather around Mom as she carefully cuts the tops off the pumpkins, making sure we have plenty of newspaper protection beneath.

Marilyn and Sharry tear into the pumpkins scraping out the seeds and guts, using large stainless steel spoons. They love that gushy feel. Linda and Marcia think it is much too yucky, and are glad to let the others do the dirty work. Mom wields the knife cutting triangles for the eyes and nose. Then she cuts jagged teeth in a nice wide smile. We keep them pretty ordinary, wonderfully traditional. Outfitted with candles, they are positioned on the stairs, ready to scare away any tricksters that might come by.

**OCT. 23**

Without meaning to scare the youngest member of the family, sometimes conversations occur that do, in fact, scare that little one. Mom has been concerned that the hoodlums, the bad boys, the bad apples in her class might try to get revenge at Halloween for all of the hard times she has given them in school. 'They will probably end up in the juvenile detention center," she laments occasionally. "They are too big and rough for fourth grade; they've been held back too many times." We say they " flunked." That's what happens when you get too many "E's". Here is the grading scale: A - great job/ perfect   B – really good  C - average     D – below average   E – unacceptable/ failing.

All of the talk about the bad boys is causing Linnie to have recurring nightmares about these boys coming on Halloween and setting fire to the grass at the corner, which is going to slowly burn up the house. In the dream, Linnie tries to wake people to warn them of the disaster, but they won't wake up. It's so scary that she wakes up crying, so Marilyn rocks her back to sleep, assuring her it isn't real, and everything is ok.

*One bad apple can spoil the whole bushel.*

**OCT. 24**

The only children who don't love school and their teachers are the ruffians. All the other children do. We can count on a steady stream of trick-or-treat-ers on Halloween, all of Mom's present *and past* students. They know where we live since most of them walk by our house on the way to school. Kris and Kres Hultman, who always act in Mom's plays, will probably have the cutest costumes; they usually do.

OCT. 25

Here is our Halloween song. It has to be sung at each doorway, or no treats are given.

*"Halloween, Halloween.*
*O what funny things are seen.*
*Witches hats, coal black cats,*
*Broomstick riders, mice and rats."*
(yell) TRICK OR TREAT!

OCT. 26

"Trick or treat!" What does it mean? It means treat me, give me a treat, (usually candy) or I'll trick you. A common trick is to write "Boo" with soap on windows, Ivory soap working the best, because it is so soft, car windows being the easiest because they can be reached. Another trick is to wrap bushes and small trees with toilet paper, called "TP-ing ". Of course, *we* never do the tricks, but we do get the treats.

[O.K., we *may* have done a few harmless tricks when we were in high school.]

OCT. 27

We collect our treats in pillowcases, and our pillowcases are bulging by the end of the evening, containing full sized Snickers, Baby Ruths, Butterfingers, Hershey bars, Tootsie Rolls, and the new Tootsie Roll Pops. Some people give us bubble gum or packs of gum that contain five sticks of gum loaded with sugar. And a few folks give us apples, nickels and pennies.

## OCT. 28

We go to the houses of people we know and trust, our neighbors, and would never think of going clear across town. Many kinds of candy are not wrapped, like candy corn and little candy pumpkins, which are standard fare. Our most favorite treat is the popcorn balls wrapped in orange cellophane given to us by the Faber sisters, spinsters who live over on Monroe Street.

## OCT. 29

Here are Mom's warnings as we head out into the night: Big girls hold the little girls' hands, especially crossing the streets. Just go to the people's houses that we know. Be sure to say "Thank you." Stay away from those big boys that shouldn't really be out because they're too old. Watch out for slippery leaves since it's been raining, and don't stay out too late. We want this to be a fun, *safe* night.

## OCT. 30

Once it gets dark, we traipse up and down the street knocking on doors, and sing our little song over and over. "Now who can these four spooky characters be?" the neighbors always say, though they probably can guess because they know us so well. "We're the Gotch girls, " Marilyn answers. She is our spokesperson. "I'm Marilyn. This is my twin sister, Marcia." "I'm Sharry," butts in Sharon. "See my cottontail?" she says, turning around. "I'm a dancer, you know. This is my dance costume." "And the little ghost in the sheet is Linda," Marilyn adds, pulling her out from behind. "Very well then. Happy Halloween to you all. Here are some nice treats." "Thank you! Happy Halloween!" we say, and move on.

## OCT. 31

Bursting in with our pillowcases full of goodies, we dump everything out in individual piles and compare our loot. Marcia is putting all of her things in nice little piles. Sharry and Marilyn are already gobbling up their favorite things, and Linnie, tired as she is from being dragged all over, is looking over her pieces with a rather blank stare.

After energetically sharing our adventures with Mom, we are reminded by her that it is well past bedtime. "Morning will be here before you know it," she warns. We climb into bed, but there is no getting to sleep after all that excitement. "You girls quiet down in there and go to sleep," shouts Dad from his bed. He had been trying to sleep through all of the hubbub. "Do I have to get my belt?" he threatens. We never want him to do that! "Come on, you guys, get quiet," Marilyn whispers. "You're getting us in trouble." "O.K., we're going to be quiet now." "Shhh." (louder) "Shhh." (louder) "Shhhh." Quiet at last, but what will November bring?

# My Halloween Memories and Fears

Chicago Tribune "Injun Summer" illustration

Mrs. Gotch   School Pictures

Linda & Sharon

Marcia          Marilyn

Sharon          Linda

Leaf Rubbing

The Twins, the Redhead, the Baby

# Chapter Three       Any November
## *Counting and Losing Count*

**NOV. 1**

November always begins with a pre-breakfast snack of Halloween candy. Within a week, Marcia and Sharon have polished theirs off. Eventually Linda's is gone as well, hastened by a little snitching from Sharon. Months later, we are likely to find a small bag of dried up candy bars stashed in the back of Marilyn's drawer; shaking our heads, we chuckle at her propensity to squirrel away food for some unforeseen emergency.

**NOV. 2**

It's beginning to get cold, moving us to dig out our winter coats, hats, mittens and gloves from the back of the closet, reminding us that Christmas is right around the corner. Let's see. What is our jingle? "Thirty days hath September... April, June, and November. All the rest have thirty-one except February twenty-eight, leap year twenty-nine." Well then, adding the twenty-eight days left in November to the twenty-four days in December makes fifty-one days until Christmas. No wonder Dad has been up at night figuring what records to buy for the Christmas season.

## NOV. 3

This is the month to count our blessings, but we have so many that we lose count. We are thankful for each other, for our parents, for our aunts and uncles who are very good to us, for our cousins. "Your family comes first," is what every Gotch believes. Grandpa Gotch preached this, and the rest of us followed. We never even met Grandpa Gotch, because he died when Dad was only nineteen, but we live out his message.

## NOV. 4

Being thankful doesn't just come naturally; it is easier to take things for granted, to wish for the things we don't have, to think the grass is greener on the other side of the fence. Mom reminds us that, though we don't have many of the fancy material things others have, we have all of the things that matter most in life, the true riches.

*The grass is always greener*
*on the other side of the fence.*

## NOV. 5

We are thankful for our little home, so cozy, so comfortable, so convenient. Every nook and cranny is packed with memories of times we have had in the past, is promising good times to be had in the future, and is serving today as the repository for all of the little possessions each one of us holds dear. What more could anyone want?

## NOV. 6

We are thankful for our faith. Being good Catholics is important to the Gotch family. Crucifixes, blessed palms, rosaries, prayer books, holy water, and statues of inspiring saints surround us. Baptisms, first communions, confirmations, weddings and funerals are important experiences we share as a family, rituals we are comfortable with and take for granted, but never think that much about or discuss.

*The family that prays together stays together.*

NOV. 7

We are thankful to be healthy and strong, so we can ride our bikes and roller skate. We get sick now and then, of course, but nothing serious, nothing that lasts. Dad has sugar diabetes and Mom has high blood pressure, but they don't seem to affect our lives very much. Marcia has a trick knee, Sharon is allergic to strawberries, and Linda is often anemic, but those things aren't very important. We have all had the mumps and three-day measles, and everyone but Marcia has had the chicken pox, but we didn't get polio during the polio epidemic, so we feel pretty lucky.

[In the polio epidemic of 1952, fifty-nine thousand cases of polio were recorded, some in every state, nearly all of them children, children who became paralyzed or died, children who could not breathe, and had to live in iron lungs, steel cylinders that kept them alive. We saw the pictures in Life magazine, and we knew of people who got it. There was a nice girl that lived by Aunt Millie who walked with a limp because of polio, and there was a girl in our school, too.]

[When Marilyn brought the chicken pox home from school, Sharry came down with them, too. She was two and a half. After Sharon had them, Linda came down with them as well, but she was only two months old. The bumps were so itchy, they had to tie her little hands into her nightgown to keep her from scratching.]

**NOV. 8**

We are thankful for our community where many people give so much of their time and energy and wisdom to help us grow. Our teachers, our neighbors, our friends, the other people in our town all encourage us in various ways to develop our strengths and overcome our weaknesses, to use our talents, to be good, to care about others, to do our part to make the world a better place, to reach for high goals, to be all we can be.

**NOV. 9**

We are thankful to be Americans, to live in a free country where we have the opportunity to stand up for what is right and good. We have written essays about citizenship for the American Legion contest, and two of us even won the award. Someday, we will be able to vote; already, we know that's important. We are proud that Dad works as a judge at the polls, ringing a bell, announcing, "The polls are now officially open," and "The polls are now officially closed."
[Following this tradition, Linda and Marcia worked for many years at the polls.]

**NOV. 10**

We are thankful to have a mother that is patient

and forgiving toward Dad, even when he lets her down, like when he has a bit too much to drink. She never antagonizes him and is not argumentative, which means we can have a peaceful home... most of the time.

*No one is perfect.*

## NOV. 11

We are thankful that Dad is so handsome and ever so playful when he is at his best. Though Dad is the uncontested authority in our family, he rarely interferes with Mom's clear ideas of how she wants to raise her girls. If we ask him if we can do something or go somewhere, he will usually respond, "Go ask your mother."

We know that Dad is probably disappointed that he didn't have any boys. Fathers always want to have sons to carry on their name, but he doesn't complain about it. If someone asks him about having all those girls, he'll usually say, " How can one man be so lucky?"

## NOV. 12

We are thankful for Saturdays. Mom loves to cook, but since she teaches school all week, Saturdays are the only days she is home to make us home cooked meals that are not just meat and potatoes and vegetables from a can. On Saturdays we have foods like halushki kapushki, and luckshaw, barbecued spare ribs, homemade vegetable soup, and liver with onions, Sharry's favorite.

Breakfasts around the breakfast nook include sour milk pancakes made with sour milk that has been sitting on the stove so long that the white solids and

the liquid are separate, pancakes so sour they kind of
bite back, pancakes loaded with butter and dark corn
syrup, pancakes so good you never want to stop eating
them. French toast is another favorite, and eggs
cooked in bacon grease. If we wake up to the smell of
bacon, we know it must be Saturday.

## NOV. 13

We are thankful for the opportunities we have
been given for dance, drum,and piano lessons, for
participation in bands and choruses, and various
classes and clubs, thankful for good friends who share
these good times with us, thankful to be exposed to
culture, to Mom's love of poetry, to concerts and plays,
in spite of the fact that we live in a rural community.
In the summer, Mom directs the children's productions
at the community theatre; we are proud of her for
doing it.

## NOV. 14

We are thankful for music, all different kinds. Both
of our parents love music, and Aunt Millie is always
teaching us to appreciate everything from Hillbilly
[now called Country and Western] to her favorite,
Classical, with many other varieties in between. We
are being taught that there is great joy in expressing
music through dance, and that there is just the right
tune to get us through pretty much any situation in
life.

## NOV. 15

We are thankful for books. Where would we be
without our beloved books? We all love to read,
to learn new things, and to discuss ideas. We are

thankful to have good minds. We like to ponder and to question, even to disagree at times, to challenge each other's opinions. Like most of the Gotch's, we have pretty strong opinions about many things. Mom and Marilyn and Linda are more the peacemakers. Sharon and Marcia like to have the last word. Of course, Dad *gets* the last word.

## NOV. 16

We are thankful that Mom and her sister, Aunt Martha, show us how sisterly love over a lifetime can be a wonderful thing in spite of many differences. They live many miles apart, have different religious beliefs (one Roman Catholic and one Protestant), have different lifestyles (one with no children, the other with four), and live at different socio-economic levels (Aunt Martha, is clearly much wealthier financially than we are). Still, they love each other and find ways to support each other.
[They had a loving supportive sister relationship to the very end of their lives.]

## NOV. 17

If we really think about it, we can be thankful that everything we ask for is not given to us. There are many "maybes" which, at our house, usually translate to "no", but only for our own good. Sometimes we are under a lot of pressure from other kids to do something we know we shouldn't do. Then we can always say, "I can't; my mom would *kill* me if she ever found out I did that!" Then they back off. There are also many "yeses" to our requests, though, because we have developed a taste for doing what is right and good, so we are thankful for that.

## NOV. 18

In school, we've been learning about the Pilgrims and the great feast they had with the Indians, which is fun to act out. The Indians teach the Pilgrims about corn, about how to use fish as fertilizer, about the delicious taste of turkey and deer meat. Of course we make turkeys by tracing around our hands. What we are thankful for doesn't fit on the four fingers which make up the tail.

## NOV. 19

Having prepared our hearts by thinking of what we are thankful for, we turn to the matter of the celebration itself. Physical preparations begin in the days before Thanksgiving Day. Since Uncle Johnny lives alone in the Big House, Aunt Tillie, his sister, comes the Saturday before to clean the house really well. If we are aware that she is there, we might go down and keep her company for a bit. She is a cheerful soul and a hard worker. It's during these times that she might break out whistling a long trilling bird song that you just cannot believe is coming from a person.

## NOV. 20

The Big House is so big and beautiful! Compared to our little house, it is a *mansion*, but it's a rather lonely place when the family isn't all there, having the stuffy smell of disuse, the air of an old library. And if you go there when it isn't a holiday, and you sit down, you immediately feel as if you should pull your skirt down over your knees. Gone are the sweet old days when Marcia and Marilyn went down to spend happy times with Grandma, the days when she was still alive. Still, we are thankful to have the Big House for our

whole family to meet in for we could never all meet in
any one of our individual homes, since they are much
too small.

NOV. 21

We walked to town today to help Mom carry
the various groceries home that will make our
contribution to the holiday meal, each one carrying
a brown paper bag, bags so heavy we had to keep
switching them from one arm to the other, bags so
heavy we had to balance them on our hips, bags, like
Linda's, that started to rip, and got progressively
worse as time went on, finally dumping out all over
the porch, the contents rolling down the stairs, as soon
as we reached home. It's good she was carrying the
sweet potatoes and not the eggs. So much work goes
into having a big celebration, but it will be worth it.
We're excited.

NOV. 22

The night before Thanksgiving, we go over to Aunt
Millie's to help prepare the stuffing. Little hands are
good at tearing up the stale bread, and the older girls
can chop celery. Mom chops the stinky onions. Aunt
Millie freely scatters the fragrant sage and thyme over
the bowlful, adding the wet stuff, and then gushes
everything together with her stubby fingers.

[It was rumored that oysters went into the mix, but
Linda never believed it, preferring to think they were
just kidding about that. When Grandma was still
alive, this same process went on right down at the Big
House.]

## NOV. 23

The women have their Thanksgiving. They cook, chat, set a beautiful table, serve a sumptuous meal, clean up, chat, laugh, serve another meal, chat, clean up the mess, go home tired and satisfied. The men have their Thanksgiving. They drink, talk sports, eat, argue politics, watch football, and fall asleep in their chairs.

## NOV. 24

We kids have our Thanksgiving. There are six of us: the four Gotch Girls and our cousins, Judy and Billy Ahearn. Billy, obviously, is very outnumbered, but he never complains. We find the two cousins very entertaining; it is a nice change for us to be around a boy. Upstairs, in Aunt Marie's girlhood bedroom, we fill the hours with quiet games. * We also might play "School" up the giant oak staircase with the oldest being the teacher (usually Marilyn).

*See Appendix C

## NOV. 25

Aunt Tillie is the first to arrive at the Big House on the big day, bringing with her the pies she has made the night before. She makes a pot of coffee in a large white porcelain pot using coffee grounds and egg shells wrapped in a tea towel. Then she peels the potatoes and gets them cooking. The twins often go down in the morning to help peel potatoes, and set the table, spreading out the long white tablecloths and getting the china and silverware from the buffet next to the dining table, setting it just so. Then, one by one, relatives with other food items arrive.

NOV. 26

Ahearns arrive next, bringing the fruit salad, the relishes, and the chocolate fudge. Aunt Millie and Uncle Jeff provide the turkey. She cooks it at home; he carries it in. "Here comes 'the Bird!'" someone calls out as they see the little Volkswagen bug pull up out front, filling the Big House with a wave of excitement. Then we all watch as Uncle Jeff's fat little body, huffing and puffing and straining under the weight of that huge turkey pan, wafts that familiar aroma past us on the way to the kitchen, amidst many oohs and ah's.

NOV. 27

Mom arrives last because her vegetable casseroles are a time-consuming work of art, consisting of golden brown scalloped corn, sweet potatoes in little pillows with perfectly placed pecans, and a tricolor cauliflower, green bean, carrot dish garnished with buttered bread crumbs.

NOV. 28

Perhaps Mom is the last one to come to the Big House because she isn't all that eager for this kind of celebration, though it is what we do *every single holiday.* Dad will have it no other way. These Big House affairs, with all of their drinking and passionate arguing, are very different, no doubt, than the holidays of her growing up years. She comes from quiet, rather stoic, religious Protestant stock, and seldom drinks alcohol herself. Though confident, she is a soft-spoken person who generally keeps her emotions in check. If she is upset, we might only know it by seeing that the blood vessel in her neck is pulsing furiously. No wonder she has had life-long high blood pressure.

[We Gotch Girls also have bittersweet memories about the holidays. We loved playing with our cousins. We loved the excitement of a big family being together, but we did not like the excessive drinking and arguing; both were a bit disturbing to us all.]

**NOV. 29**

Sitting down to the meal in our customary seats, grownups around the big dining room table, children at the card table, we get sprinkled with holy water by Aunt Millie who then leads the grace. We all know it by heart and say it together out loud. "Bless us O Lord, and these Thy gifts which we are about to receive, from Thy bounty, through Christ Our Lord, Amen." From the head of the table, Uncle Johnny, as patriarch of the family, proclaims, "Commence!" and we all dig in.

**NOV. 30**

At the kids' table, we pile our plates high, thinking we can eat it all, but we rarely do. Our eyes are always bigger than our stomachs, and we are eager to get on with the games. Billy is the exception. He can eat two plates full, and follow it with pumpkin pie. For a skinny kid, he can eat an enormous amount of food. At one summer cookout, he ate thirteen ears of corn.

*Looks like your eyes were bigger than your stomach.*

This holiday ends, but another big one is right around the corner.

## The Big House

Thanks for so
many blessings!

American Legion Award

*Holiday Time with cousins in Hebron*

*First Communion Photos*

# Chapter Four      Any December
## *Music in the Air*

**DEC. 1**      *Silver Bells*    by Bing Crosby 1950
"And on every street corner you hear..." music from
the Gotch Radio Specialties. Uncle Jerry runs our
Music in the Air Program, piped from the loudspeaker
system atop our warehouse building. It's magical. We
can't hear it inside the store, but it can be heard all up
and down Main Street. Streator's whole downtown is
alive with the sounds of Christmas.

         24 DAYS 'TIL CHRISTMAS


**DEC. 2**    *It's Beginning to Look A Lot Like Christmas*
         by Bing Crosby   1951

"It's beginning to look a lot like Christmas..."
already. Instead of turkeys, pumpkins, and
cornucopias hanging in the record department, we

now have reindeer, snowflakes, Christmas trees, ornaments, and, of course, Santas. The record department window shelf is decorated with a glorious snow scene. The front display window has been sprayed with real plastic snow. Beautiful white painted branches covered with glitter, the ones we helped Mom make last fall, are part of the window display. Our three foot high RCA Victor dog, Nipper, is there dressed in a red Santa hat. Everything sparkles and our hearts are filled with the excitement of the season.

23 DAYS 'TIL CHRISTMAS


DEC. 3        *Jingle Bells*

"Dashing through the snow..." we sing over and over tonight as Sharon and Linda are making paper chain garlands for the Christmas tree with red and green construction paper tabs, sticking them together with library paste. It's fun to see them grow in length. They go faster than the popcorn ones the twins are stringing with needles and long pieces of thread. We've never dashed through the snow in a one horse open sleigh, but it's still fun to sing. Mom is with us grading papers, as usual.

22 DAYS 'TIL CHRISTMAS


DEC. 4     *Santa Claus is Comin' to Town*
                  by Bing Crosby 1950

"He knows if you've been bad or good..." We all have the pre-Christmas jitters. We know we've been

naughty as well as nice. When Aunt Martha called
and asked Mom if we girls had been good or not, she
said, "Yes, very good," but did she really mean it? We
haven't *always* been good. We sometimes pouted and
cried. We found it difficult to go to sleep at night.
Would Santa have seen all of that, and maybe decide
not to come, or give us a lump of coal instead of the
gifts we asked him to bring? These are the questions
that go through our minds this time of year.

21 DAYS 'TIL CHRISTMAS

DEC. 5 *The Chipmunks*
by David Seville 1958

"Christmas time is here again..." schoolwork falls
behind again. We don't want to be in school anymore
now; we want vacation. We don't want arithmetic
problems, spelling lists, book reports and all that stuff
Mom calls "busywork."

It's hard to wait. Since the chipmunk song came out,
we're all talking and singing like chipmunks. It's silly
and fun.

20 DAYS 'TIL CHRISTMAS

DEC. 6 *I Saw Mommy Kissing Santa Claus*
by Jimmy Boyd 1952

"Underneath the mistletoe last night..." Since
this song came out in 1952 we have loved the *I Saw
Mommy Kissing Santa Claus* song. Actually, we
never did see Mommy kissing Santa Claus. We saw
Santa Claus when he came to visit the Big House on

Christmas Eve, but Mom was never kissing him. Dad was there, too. Some things are hard to understand. We have never had a chimney for him to come down either, but somehow he gets the presents under our tree.

19 DAYS 'TIL CHRISTMAS

DEC. 7     *Rockin' Around the Christmas Tree*
by Brenda Lee 1958
"Rockin' around the...record shop, have a happy holiday." While we are working at the shop, we love to put this tune on the demo phonograph and rock around for a while. We have to wait until Aunt Millie is out to Kresge's having lunch. She isn't crazy about us dancing in the store, but business is slow at lunchtime, and Dad never really said we couldn't dance at the store; he is gone anyway. If a customer comes in we can easily flip off the music, pop back into our professional mode, and ask, "May we help you?"

18 DAYS 'TIL CHRISTMAS

DEC. 8     *I'll Be Home for Christmas*
by Elvis Presley 1957

"I'll be home for Christmas.... if only in my dreams" Aunt Martha called again, as she often does. After talking quietly for a bit, Mom got off the phone, and we could see that she had tears in her eyes. Perhaps they talked about Christmases past and missed being together. She misses her family sometimes, especially around the holidays. "But," she says, longingly, "that is just the way it has to be," knowing we can not travel to see them very often, for sixty miles is a long way to go these days. Besides, it wouldn't be Christmas if we weren't at the Big House. Each of us took turns wishing Aunt Martha a Merry Christmas. Aunt Martha told Mom that our wishes meant a lot to her. In many ways, we are her girls, too.                    17 DAYS 'TIL CHRISTMAS

DEC. 9          *White Christmas*
                         by Bing Crosby   1942

"I'm dreaming of a white Christmas... just like the ones I used to know." So far the snow hasn't come this year, but we hope it comes soon. Snow helps people get into the Christmas spirit, the spirit to get their Christmas shopping done. We haven't been too busy at the store, but we aren't into the last two weeks yet.

Mom's been trying to write out Christmas cards to all of our far-away friends, a little each night, but that, too, is more difficult to do if it's not white outside. The Christmas card from Mom's friend that lives in Tehran, Iran came today. She sends one every year that is hand painted and drawn in ink. Usually it is a picture of her growing family where they live, with palm trees and camels. They really have to dream of a white Christmas!

                         16 DAYS 'TIL CHRISTMAS

DEC. 10         *The Christmas Song*
                         by Nat King Cole  1953

"Chestnuts roasting on an open fire..." What are chestnuts anyway? We have never had any, but the other foods of Christmas are a delight to us, and we're always hungry. Aunt Millie brought one of her tins of homemade Christmas cookies to the shop. We devoured them in one day. We are usually too busy working at the store during Christmas to do much baking. Because Dad is a diabetic, we rarely have baked goods around the house, anyway, and if we do, they never have frosting. That's just the way it is at our house.

15 DAYS 'TIL CHRISTMAS

DEC. 11          *Here Comes Santa Claus*
                    by  Gene Autry   1947

"Here comes Santa Claus. Here comes Santa Clause..." right to the Elks Club Christmas party, where we are able to sit on his lap and tell him what we want for Christmas. Ho! Ho! Ho! He made no promises. It's a lot of fun, partly because we know most of the other kids there. Every year we are given a red mesh stocking full of hard candy and trinkets of one sort or another. Mom says they are a little chintzy, junk made in China, which they surely are, but we love them anyway. These stockings are the only ones we receive; since we don't have a fireplace at home, it's not part of our tradition. We each also receive a larger present, sometimes it is a boxed tea set wrapped in cellophane, one time a doll diaper bag. The boys get model airplanes or racing cars.

14 DAYS 'TIL CHRISTMAS

**DEC. 12**     *Let it Snow, Let it Snow, Let it Snow*
                                    1945

"Let it Snow, Let it Snow, Let it Snow... " Linda has
been playing this song over and over on the piano. I
guess it worked because it snowed last night. We woke
up to a nice white cover outside and more coming
down. Perfect, because it's Saturday. Since we were
up early, we all went out to make a snowman before
breakfast. It was that good heavy wet snow that packs
so well. The twins made the bottom. Sharry made the
middle, and Linda made the little head. After breakfast, the twins went to work at the shop with Dad. He
was whistling Christmas carols; maybe it will be a
good season after all.     13 DAYS 'TIL CHRISTMAS

**DEC. 13**     *Suzy Snowflake*
                        by Rosemary Clooney 1951

"Here comes Suzy Snowflake... look at her tumbling down, tap, tap, tapping at your window pane to
tell you she's in town." The snow is very sparkly and
beautiful. Everyone is happy because the snow means
we'll probably have a white Christmas. The shop had
one of the best days ever yesterday.

We went to Mass this morning grateful. After
Sunday dinner, Sharon and Linda made paper snowflakes, every one different, just like the real ones.
Mom says we girls are like the snowflakes, no two
alike. We have a hard time not comparing ourselves to
each other, but that's exactly what she *doesn't* want us
to do.     12 DAYS 'TIL CHRISTMAS

DEC. 14          *O Tannenbaum*
by Fred Waring
and the Pennsylvanians
"O Tannenbaum, O Tannenbaum..." We
put the Christmas tree up today after school. We
could hardly wait to get home to do it. As soon as we
brought the tree into the house, we had to find and
play " O Tannenbaum." We played it again and again
as we decorated the tree, putting on the chains we
had made and all of the ornaments, including strings
of tinsel. Mom sings it in German, with tears in her
eyes. All of us were sobbing by the time we had placed
our last ornament. *We* cry because *she* cries, perhaps
we're missing the German grandmother we never
knew.          11 DAYS 'TIL CHRISTMAS


DEC. 15     *Have Yourself a Merry Little Christmas*
by Judy Garland, 1944


"Have yourself a merry little Christmas..." In Mom's
German Christmas tradition, the tree never came
until Christmas day. Santa brought it that morning.
Every year Mom tells us how great it was to have Santa bring the tree. "Why doesn't Santa bring our tree?"
we often wonder. We'll have a merry little Christmas
even if we get our tree from the Christmas tree lot.
Our store is open every night until 9 pm these last two
weeks. We've been busy.
10 DAYS 'TIL CHRISTMAS

*You have to make hay while the sun shines*
*and get while the gettin's good.*


— 79 —

DEC. 16        *A Marshmallow World*
by Bing Crosby   1950

"It's a Marshmallow World", that means more
snow, just what we need. We girls are doing a lot of
shoveling on these snowy days, taking turns. It's so
great, so Christmassy! Wish we had time to make
more snowmen, but we're lucky to get our homework
done while we're working at the store after school
until nine. These days are pretty long, but just two
more days and school will be out.

9 DAYS 'TIL CHRISTMAS

DEC. 17        *Jolly Ole St. Nicholas*

Dad has been a "jolly ole St. Nicholas" lately.
Business is booming, and that always makes him
happy. We love that joyful Dad. Tired as we all were,
when *Mele Kalikimaka* was playing on the phonograph
at home tonight, he danced Mom around the living
room a little bit. We haven't seen that before! They
used to go dancing every Saturday night when they
were dating, but that seems like a million years ago.
He hasn't said it in so many words, but we know he
loves and is proud of his "Gotch Girls", the way we
pitch in and are good workers.

8 DAYS 'TIL CHRISTMAS

**DEC. 18**        *Joy to the World*

" Joy to the World, the Lord is come..." We were
joyful today singing all of the Christmas carols at
the school program. We did *Joy to the World, Hark
the Herald Angels Sing, O Little Town of Bethlehem,*
and *O Holy Night,* which are all so beautiful, and the
fun ones like *Jingle Bells* and *Rudolph the Red-nosed
Reindeer,* too. Finally, it's the last day of school before
vacation!  Yea!        7 DAYS 'TIL CHRISTMAS


**DEC. 19**        *Jingle Bell Rock*
                   by Teresa Brewer 1958
    "Jingle Bell, Jingle Bell, Jingle Bell Rock"... we
were rockin' at the store today. The Saturday before
Christmas is always the biggest day of the year. The
snow was just what we needed to get everyone going
in terms of shopping. We were so busy, we didn't get a
break to eat until almost eight o'clock; all of a sudden,
we were famished. Slipping out the back door and
through the alley to Dutch's Tavern to buy potato
chips and Italian hot beef sandwiches is so much a
part of our work routine this time of year that it's
become part of our holiday celebration. That sandwich
really hits the spot!
                          6 DAYS 'TIL CHRISTMAS


*That really hits the spot!*
*(Said of a welcome drink or meal.)*

DEC. 20    *Adeste Fideles*
              by The Harry Simeone Chorale

"Adeste Fideles laeti triumphantes..." It's Sunday.
The store is closed. We often sing and say Latin in
church with only the faintest idea of what it means.
Something honoring to God we trust. At any rate, it
always sounds quite lovely and churchy. The church
is beautifully decorated for Christmas and looks
lovely even without the Christmas decorations. The
manger is in the corner, reminding us of the real
reason for Christmas. Many candles have been lit as
people remember their dead family members who are
not with them this holiday season, which makes the
church extra full of twinkles.

                          5 DAYS 'TIL CHRISTMAS

DEC. 21    *God Rest Ye Merry Gentlemen*

          "O tidings of comfort and joy, comfort
and joy..." Not the important tidings of Christ coming
to the earth, but Aunt Millie announced the tidings
today that all of the special orders have now arrived.
Those are good tidings, too, because it means all of
the customers will have them for Christmas. We were
busy all day! Looks like many people are giving the
"gift that keeps on giving", as we call it, music.
    Aunt Millie always sits down at the end of a day
like this and says, "Oh, my dogs are tired!" She says
"dogs" but we all know she means her feet. She always
wears her black "old lady shoes," but they don't seem
to help. From nine in the morning until nine at night
is a long time to be on your feet.

                          4 DAYS 'TIL CHRISTMAS

*Give the gift of music, the gift that keeps on giving.*

DEC. 22     *"Twas the Night Before Christmas"*
Read by Perry Como

"'Twas the Night Before Christmas and All
Through the Night" We heard Perry Como reading
this on the radio today and realized that although
it isn't the night before, it's almost the night before,
and we have been so busy helping other people buy
just the right gift for the ones they love, that we
haven't finished our own Christmas shopping, so we
took turns today going out picking up the things we
needed, for we always buy each other and Mom and
Dad a little something at least. The twins usually
go together on their gifts, and Linda and Sharon go
together. We have our own money that we have been
saving all year at the bank in our Christmas club. We
put twenty-five cents in each week, so we each have
twelve dollars to spend, which should be enough for
all of our gifts. The gifts will be small, but it's the
thought that counts.

3 DAYS 'TIL CHRISTMAS

*It's the thought that counts.*

DEC. 23     *We Wish You a Merry Christmas*

"We wish you a Merry Christmas..." We bought a
little package of hankies for Auntie Florence today,

— 83 —

our friend who lives just up the street, the one who makes pretty flowers out of napkins and tissue paper. ( She even taught us how to do it one time.) She'll probably come over after Christmas with a box of eight crayons for each of us like she usually does.

Even though she is not really our aunt, she has a great fondness for the twins because she helped Mom take care of them when they were babies. Auntie Florence is very old and lives on just a little money. We think it is wonderfully thoughtful of her to give us *anything,* even if it is just eight crayons.

2 DAYS 'TIL CHRISTMAS

DEC. 24   CHRISTMAS EVE
*Silent Night*
by  Bing Crosby   1935

"Silent Night, Holy Night..." Eventually, we will get to a silent and holy night, but much activity comes first. *At last,* Christmas Eve has arrived. By 5:30 or so, the last stragglers getting those last-minute gifts are finally gone. After locking up, we gather in the repair shop with a few friends to have a little holiday cheer. Mom has made some meat roll-ups and Ritz crackers with cheese. Gathering outside the back door, we play the last of the Music in the Air, Mario Lanza singing *Ave Maria* and *The Lord's Prayer.* A few snow flakes are drifting down. Aunt Millie and all the rest of us are in tears at the beauty of it all.  Dad passes out envelopes with a little Christmas bonus for each of us.

Once we are home, we have a little rest, and maybe open a special gift from Mom and Dad. Wild with

excitement, we head down to the Big House, where
the rest of the family is gathered, for more festivities.
In a bit, Santa Claus might come. If he doesn't, one of
his helpers, an aunt or uncle, begins distributing gifts
from the gigantic pile under the Christmas tree that
is set up in front of the bay window of the living room.
Looks like all of the men received socks and ties again
this year. You can tell by the size of the package.
Aunt Millie loves to buy us dolls. Walking dolls, who
can walk along side of you, the "I Love Lucy" baby
Rickey doll, who is the actual size of a real live baby
and comes with real baby clothes; and Linda's rag
doll, Hildegard are some of the ones we have received.
One year Santa Claus brought us our Tiny Tears
dolls, who take a bottle of water, and then wet their
pants, cry real tears, and have fuzzy hair that you can
shampoo. Billy always receives sports related games,
which seem more interesting to Sharry than the dolls
we get. One year he got a wood burning set, and that
fascinated all of us.

After all of the hoopla of the gifts, we make our way
to the church for Midnight Mass, out into the dark
silent night to think about the One whose birthday we
are celebrating. As the priest drones away, many little
heads nod off. Some bigger heads, too, if they have
been having a little too much holiday cheer. Back out
in the cold night air, we revive just enough to enjoy
a bowl of Slovakian wild mushroom and sauerkraut
soup back at the Big House before collapsing into bed
for a few hours before the Main Event.

1 DAY 'TIL CHRISTMAS

DEC. 25  CHRISTMAS DAY!
*Here We Come A-caroling*
by the New Christy Minstrels

"Here we come a-caroling"...Without fail, we always
find presents under the tree on Christmas morning,
many presents, just the presents we have dreamed of
and asked Santa for, mostly unwrapped so we can dig
right in playing with them.  Sharry is always up first,
rousting the rest of us.  We play with our toys and eat
rushka while Mom prepares the vegetables, until we
head down to the Big House for the next tradition of
the day, the feast.  After the meal, the afternoon will
be spent playing games, especially fun if we have
received new board games.  Eventually, with Aunt
Millie coaching and corralling us, we will slip out the
back door, and go around to the front, ringing the
doorbell as if we are perfect strangers.  We cousins
sing the traditional songs, as well as the Slovak
Christmas song we call "Povatsana" and then pass
a hat, into which the uncles throw money.  The more
money we see, the louder we sing.  After the caroling,
and a little more pie, we all go home richer in many
ways.

[When Linnie, the baby of the family, was just 5
or 6, she sang a solo of "Christmas is a Coming and
the Goose is Getting Fat."  Of course, that was a big
hit.  Uncle Jerry recorded it, but, unfortunately, the
recording has been lost.]

CHRISTMAS AT LAST

DEC. 26
Christmas vacation officially begins for the younger

girls today. We sleep late and can stay in our PJ's all
morning. Play is our only agenda. We can tell Mom
enjoys being home as well. Marilyn fastidiously puts
all of her toys away so none of them will get broken.
Then she plays with ours. No wonder in the weeks
to come hers will make a re-appearance and be
beautifully brand new. The twins need to help out at
the store today, as customers will be bringing records
back for one reason or another, duplicate gifts and
such. Some customers will be shopping with their
gift certificates. We continue to play our Christmas
records at home, but the Music in the Air is done for
the season. We hate the thought of Christmas coming
to an end.


DEC. 27

Finally Dad gets to take a day off, since it's Sunday.
Though he hasn't done all of the figuring yet, it
seemed to be a really good season. "Let's go for a
drive up to Oak Hills, and see how the other half
lives," someone suggested. We like to see the beautiful
Christmas decorations they have lit up all over their
yards in the ritzy part of town, one more beautiful
than the next. We don't do that in our neighborhood.
We like to take a drive up there at least once during
the season, and we haven't had time to so far. A light
snow is falling, which makes looking in the windows
all the more lovely.


DEC. 28

Like many other folks this time of year, we have
to take some of the gifts back that we have received

for Christmas, so we walked to town. The sun was
back out this morning, so the shoveled sidewalks
were safely dry. We stopped in JCPenney to see Aunt
Tillie. The mezzanine floor where she sells fabric
was dead as a doornail today. With the holidays and
everything, I guess everyone is too busy to sit and sew.
They really sold a lot before Christmas, though, as
ladies were making Christmas gifts and sewing new
decorations for their homes.

**DEC. 29**
Everyone who walked into our store today wanted to
know if we had had a Merry Christmas. There weren't
many customers, so we could be more relaxed and visit
with them. That was nice. Already it was beginning to
feel a lot *not* like Christmas.

**DEC. 30**
Aunt Millie reminded us how to do inventory today.
We have to count every record in the shop. We do
this every year, so Dad can figure up the numbers for
taxes. We work together in pairs, getting our little
systems going. It still seems to take forever.

**DEC. 31**      *Auld Lang Syne*
                    by Guy Lombardo     1953

Today we dismantled the Christmas decorations,
and Christmas disappeared for another year. We
delivered the packages of unsold records to the post

office for shipment, back to RCA and Columbia and Decca Records. Our backs ached at the end of the day just thinking about all those heavy loads we had delivered. Everyone we passed had a "Happy New Year" greeting for us.

Dad started celebrating early with a few toasts. We mostly don't go anywhere for the evening. Mom doesn't want us to be out on the roads with people who have been drinking too much. If we can stay awake, we'll go out on the front porch in cone-shaped hats, crank our noisemakers, blow our paper roll–outs, bang on pots and pans, and shout "Happy New Year!" to everybody and nobody. We wonder what the new year will bring.

Marie, Millie, Frank,
Jerry, Tillie, Pauline, Johnnie

Winter Twins

*Elks Club*
*Christmas*
*Party*

The Cousins

A little gift...

The Gotch Clan w/ Steve & Ruie

# Merry Christmas and Happy New Year !

Tiny Tears

The Carolers

— 91 —

## Chapter Five

## Talking Walls

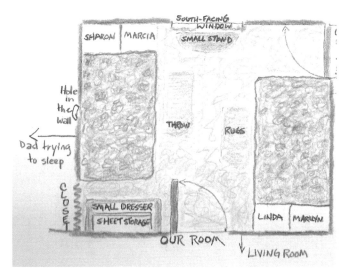

January, a month for dreaming, scheming, and re-flecting. Four girls are growing up together within the 10 x 12' walls of one bedroom. How many stories those walls could tell! What if those walls could talk? For fun, let's see what they would say.

### JAN. 1

Q: How do you look? What sort of décor do you pro-vide?

A: A bedroom for four girls *has* to be pink, of course. We are bright pink, with the latest trend in texture, a sort of stucco finish that is like bumpy sandpaper. It's only a problem when a pillow fight or other tussling leads to a bloody scrape. The floors are covered with linoleum patterned to look like carpeting, as most bedrooms are these days. Somewhere along the way, the door has lost its doorknob and hardware, which the girls find very handy for quick entry and exits, especially when one is chasing the other.

We walls have the following simple adornment: a crucifix over each bed that is draped in woven palm leaves after Palm Sunday, a framed "Now I Lay Me Down to Sleep" prayer, and a light bulb hanging from a chain in the middle of the room, sufficient light for most activities, a light which will change to a small ceiling fixture eventually. In the morning, though, light streams through the Venetian blinds of the South-facing window to waken the four little sleepyheads. What could be a better way to wake up? The best décor? The love and laughter that inhabits this little room most of the time. The girls love this little room; "our room" they call it, a room all their own.

## JAN. 2

Q: Tell us about the mysterious hole in the wall.

A: Next to Sharon and Marcia's bed there is a mysterious hole in the wall, just above the level of the bed, about halfway down. No one knows the origin of this hole, and we are not about to tell. It was a small hole until little fingers picked at the plaster month-by-month, year-by-year, as it has become the perfect mindless fiddling place for when the girls are daydreaming or are just about ready to fall asleep.

One year, in an attempt to fix it, their mother put some plaster of Paris in the hole, which had grown from the size of a hand to the size of a foot. This patch has never been painted, though, so now it is a *white* hole, drawing the fiddlers to continue their quest to pick out just a few more fragments. The girls seem to have no embarrassment about this friendly hole, this old friend of a hole. Besides, it isn't like it is in a place where you could cover it with a dresser or something.

[Perhaps it is there to this day.]

JAN. 3
Q: Four girls in one bedroom. Is there any order at all, or just chaos?

A: Oh, yes, there is *some* order, order certainly as a relative term. The clean sheets and ironed pillowcases are generally stored on top of the dresser in this room, there behind the door. The girls each have one dresser drawer of their own. The big girls have the larger closet which has a bar about four feet long for dresses, and one about two feet long for bulky items like winter coats. It is full to overflowing, with an over-the-door metal hanger full as well. Hats go up above on the shelf.

The little girls have the smaller closet that contains one bar about three feet long and some orange crates on the floor in which Sharon protectively stores her baseball cards, glove, and baseball, as well as her religious prayer cards. That small closet unfortunately has the disadvantage of having no light in it, so they keep a flashlight handy, which is more fun than a light anyway. Tucked neatly under their pillows each morning are the girls' pajamas or nightgown, so they can be found that night. Shoes for all of the girls are stored under the beds, Marcia and Sharon's under their bed, and Marilyn and Linda's under theirs. Stuffed animals and dolls are either on the bed, if

someone has made it (the big girls are *supposed* to
do this), on the floor, or on the little wooden stand.
Among them are several autograph hounds and Linda's stuffed animal skunk, named Flower, from Walt
Disney's movie, *Bambi*.

All books belong out in the living room on one of the
bookcases, and all miscellaneous toys are kept in the
basement, which acts as a playroom, furnace room,
laundry room, storage room, and cat box. Now you
know where everything *belongs*. Do four busy girls
always keep them there? No, of course not.

*A place for everything, and everything in its place,*
*just as it should be.*

## JAN. 4

Q: Tell us about the Gotch girls and their shoes?

A: In this area, the girls are definitely their mother's
daughters. They all just love having the right shoes for
the right occasion and the right outfit. Like we said,
all of the shoes are stored under the beds, with the
boots migrating to the floor of the closet in the summer. At any given time, you can find old Mary Jane's,
new Mary Jane's, tennis shoes, sandals, bedroom
slippers, snow boots, and eventually high heels, saddle
shoes, and loafers, some in various colors, for each of
the four girls. That makes for a lot of shoes under the
beds, and chaos! The girls get a bit dusty if they have
to crawl all the way to the back to get the one they
are searching for, but it is there *somewhere*, almost
always. The only time it is a big problem is Sunday
morning when they are already late for church and
one of the Mary Jane's can't be found.

[When the younger two girls were in high school, the mom and three of the girls all wore the same size shoes, 9AA, (narrow). In a pinch, they could wear each other's shoes, which was handy. Marilyn was the exception. She wore a 9, but her feet were much wider].

JAN. 5
Q: Whose job is it to clean the room?

A: Everyone has to pitch in together. Like most busy girls, they may have multiple clothing changes per day. These clothes tend to end up in piles at the ends of the beds. If it's *your* clothes on the bed, *you* have to hang them up or put them away in the drawer. This can be a real bone of contention. Marilyn and Sharon usually use the quick method of disposing of things, stuffing them in drawers randomly or tossing them all down the clothes chute to be washed. Marcia and Linda are more likely to methodically put them neatly away, organizing the drawer in the process, taking their time, often getting distracted in some way, and never finishing the job. This leads to strife. Once, after warning Marcia several times to get her clothes put away *or else*, Sharon gathered up all of Marcia's things and threw them out on the lawn. That was one way to deal with it.

JAN. 6
Q: What can be counted on to bring gales of laughter?

A: Occasionally, maybe once a year or so, there has been enough squirming around in bed, or bouncing on the bed, or rolling over, that the slats that hold the springs in place on Marilyn and Linda's bed will have moved just enough out of position that the whole bed, springs, mattress, covers and kids, will go crashing to the floor, bringing shrieks of surprise, and gales of laughter. It is like a time bomb because there is no telling exactly when such a happening will occur. It can even be in the middle of the night!

Correcting the situation is quite an ordeal...getting the bodies out, the covers and wobbly mattress off, the dusty open metal bedsprings off and then repositioning the slats, getting everything put back, completely remaking the bed, and recovering from all the disruption. It isn't easy, but then they are always going back to sleep with that wonderful feeling one gets after a really hard laugh.

**JAN. 7**

Q: Have you had any other silly accidents?

A: When the twins were small, they liked to roll their little bodies from the top of the bed to the bottom and then back again, over and over. As they rolled, they would inch further and further off the bed. One time, as Marcia inched closer and closer to the edge, she actually fell off. Unfortunately the rocking chair with the missing arm was just in the wrong place, causing a gash in her back.

[The scar is still there to prove it. Silly fun sometimes goes awry.]

Another time, one evening, when everyone was older, both parents were gone; the twins were in charge. The evening had been fairly uneventful until it was getting late. The younger two were already ready for bed, and Marilyn was tired from the long day, so she plopped herself down on the couch. Ouch! Someone had let the scissors slip down into the space between the cushions, and then had left them there. Like a sword, they inserted themselves *deeply* right into Marilyn's butt cheek. About that time, fortunately, the folks arrived back home, for the injury required a trip to the hospital for stitches. After that, the girls were a lot more careful to put the scissors away!

**JAN. 8**
Q: Did you see anything particularly unusual?

A: Oh yes. We think it is unusual for Sharry to bite her toenails the way she bites her fingernails. She is agile from all of her dancing, so that makes it easy, easier and quicker than going to get the scissors or clipper, we suppose. She always seems to go for the fastest way to do things if it is something mundane. Of course, she is reprimanded for using such an unsanitary method, but what can you do?

**JAN. 9**
Q: We know the girls giggle a great deal when they are supposed to be sleeping. What do they think is particularly funny?

A: Passing gas, of course.
   Linnie can do an amazingly accurate imitation of their father leaning way over to "let one go" at the dinner table. The other girls are marvelously entertained into gales of laughter. It is followed by an imitation of their mother's look of horror and disapproval, as she

says, "Frank!" as if it were the first time it had ever happened, and she was shocked by his lack of civility.

On the night that the girls have had lentil or butter bean soup for lunch, we walls have a particularly long evening. With four girls producing what they call "stinkers," it is just one after the other. Of course, no one ever owns up to them, so they all blame poor Hildegard, Linda's rag doll. Hildegard obviously has a real problem!

Their silly rhyme for this situation:

> *Beans, beans, the musical fruit,*
> *The more you eat, the more you toot.*
> *The more you toot, the better you feel,*
> *So eat the beans at every meal.*

## JAN. 10

Q: You must have seen a great deal of training and correcting over the years to tame these rather wild girls. What are some of the constant reminders you overheard?

A: Yes, indeed.

"Marcia, *please* don't crack your gum. You will never make a good impression as long as you are cracking your gum like that."

"Marilyn, I'm not going to let you go anywhere like that; it's just too sloppy. Fix yourself up. At least tuck in your shirt."

"Sharry, if you don't stop cracking your knuckles, you

are going to have big sore knuckles like your Aunt Millie when you get old. And it doesn't look very lady-like, either."

"Linda, if I've told you once, I've told you a hundred times, please sit still and stop kicking under the table. And remember to bring your sweater back home with you. I believe you would lose your head if it wasn't attached."

She is a real stickler for having them use correct English, too. "'Ain't' is not a word in the dictionary," she reminds them often.
[It *is* a word in the dictionary now, though.]

"You girls," their mother says, shaking her head. "What am I going to *do* with you?"

JAN. 11
Q: "You're only young once, but you are grown up for a long, long time. Stay young as long as you can." We know that is their mother's advice, but what are some things you heard them complain about that they can't do *yet*?

A:
1) Can't wear nylons and high heels until high school

2) Can't wear lipstick until high school   (They may try a little Tangee in junior high.)

3) Can't go out on dates until high school.   Once they are old enough for dating, they are not supposed to go out with boys that are older than they are.

[We all married guys who are older than we are. Maybe we didn't follow this rule very well.]

4) Can't drive the car, indefinitely.

[Marilyn went driving with Dad once, but she pushed on the gas instead of the brake, ending up in a cornfield. That was it for the rest of us. "You can learn to drive when you are old enough to buy your own car" was Dad's response to the problem.]

[Mom never learned to drive. Although all four girls eventually procured licenses, the twins were never comfortable driving, and rarely did it. Sharon only drove until she married, letting her husband be the chauffeur after that. Linda is the only one to love it, but she didn't drive until the age of twenty-three, after she was married and her husband insisted that she be more independent.]

### JAN. 12 MOM'S BIRTHDAY
Q: What would usually happen as a result of the girls' mother having a birthday?

A: Their mother doesn't usually seek the spotlight, preferring to focus attention on others. The quiet confidence she has in herself seems to make attention unnecessary, but the girls definitely remember her birthday and celebrate it in their own unique ways. The twins, being older, and having access to the bits of money they earn from working at the store, often buy her a present, something pretty, like a new pink housecoat from Kristal's clothing store with snaps down the front and some flowers embroidered on the pockets. This is a welcome gift because Hulda usually wears this kind of thing when she is at home. Sharon will try to be on her best behavior for the whole day, not even once sticking out her tongue and wrinkling her nose the way she does when she doesn't like something. That, in itself, will be a very thoughtful and appreciated gift. Linda will always make some little gift, perhaps a set of potholders made with the loom she received for Christmas. They often make her homemade birthday cards using decorations cut out of the recent Christmas cards.

**JAN. 13**
Q: How difficult do you think it is for the girls to get to sleep, four in the room, two in each bed?

A: Usually they are surprisingly good at going to sleep. Often, they quietly scratch each other's backs or tickle arms. Arms are so ticklish right where you bend at the elbow and on the inside of your wrist! Sometimes they play quiet little games like trying to guess what letter of the alphabet or number they have drawn on each other 's backs. Eventually they turn back to back and doze off.

**JAN. 14**
Q: Bet you walls are in on some pretty regular scheming. Tell about that.

A: As a rule, Marilyn shares with Marcia what they are going to do, where they are going to go, with whom, and when Marcia is to be ready. She knows Marcia will procrastinate and primp too long, but

Marilyn tries to move them along through the day in an orderly fashion. It is usually an uphill battle, as Marcia has her own agenda and timetable.

In general play, Sharon calls the shots for the younger two. She is full of plans, and Linda is happy to follow along. The one exception is when they play Madame Alexander dolls. Linda knows just what social function the dolls ought to attend and how they should be dressed. In this one area, Sharon follows.

**JAN. 15**

Q: I suppose the bedroom serves as the changing room as well as the room to sleep in. What is the result of that?

A: The older girls are very free and open when they are changing clothes down to their bare skin. In this way, the little girls are learning what they might look like in a few years. Living in such a small space and the fact that they are all girls certainly influences this openness.

[When Linda was little she would sometimes put on one of the twins' bras, stuff it with socks and look in the mirror sideways to see how she looked. It's not easy being the last one to grow up! The Gotch Girls are fairly well endowed with good-sized "bosoms" as Mom called them. She herself was quite large. While others wore padded bras and "falsies" to look like they had something, we really *had*□omething, thanks, *probably,* to our mother's good genes.]

[The older girls' openness lead to increased modesty on the part of the younger two, who generally shy away from exposure. Then again, Linda went through

a phase of wearing sexy clothing when she was a teen-
ager, and Sharon *said* she did some nude modeling for
the art department in college to pick up a few dollars.
But did she? Sharry likes to make up lies that make
her boring life sound more interesting and wild than it
is. The last thing she would have wanted was to be a
nude model.]

**JAN. 16**
Q: Any other tidbits along this line?

A: Yes, other education at this level occurs coinci-
dentally when the girls happen to notice the couple
next door chasing each other around the house. Since
the houses are identical and the windows match up
perfectly, a lit house at night with the shades open
becomes quite a movie screen. Fortunately they can
only see the dining room, and only above the waist,
but that is plenty! He has such a hairy chest and back,
so unlike their father! Such a shocking sight leads to
much blushing and giggling and conjecture!

[Dad would crack down on too much hilarity, though
he would have no idea what was so funny. Wonder
what he would have done had he known! Certainly Mom would not have approved of such late night
viewing, but realizing the reverse could happen, it was
a good reminder to us to keep the blinds closed if we
were changing our clothes.]

**JAN. 17**
Q: On a rather frivolous note, who sleeps the most?

A: Marilyn wins hands down. She loves to sleep,

falling sound asleep so quickly compared to the rest of the girls! She often sings them a lullaby, usually *The Loveliest Night of the Year*, using her lovely sweet voice. Then she'll rock the bed a little bit for Linnie, because that is what Linnie likes. Moments later, she will be sleeping like a log. Sharon is the most fitful sleeper, tossing and turning, kicking and stealing all the covers. What a mess their bed is in the morning! Marcia gets the gold star for sleeping with Sharon! Linda just tucks her little self in next to Marilyn's big, soft, warm body, snuggling herself to sleep. This obviously works out better in winter, when there is no heat in the room, than in summer when it is hot and sticky.

[We have been asked why we didn't at least have bunk beds, but all of us agree that we have no recollection of being unhappy with our sleeping arrangement. On the contrary, we look back to those times with great fondness. Because the bedrooms were not heated, they were quite chilly on winter mornings, so we would often bring our clothes and dress standing over the heat register in the kitchen, which was quite toasty.]

JAN. 18
Q: Is anything hard for you to hear?

A: Marcia sits on the edge of the bed to practice her saxophone, the same passage over and over and over. That isn't so easy, especially when she squeaks the notes. Fortunately it doesn't last very long nor occur very frequently.

Sharry's temper tantrums were the worst. How she could kick and scream and flail her arms around! It was scary, even for us. Of course there was nothing we could do about it. It was good she finally outgrew it. Her parents were probably very grateful to see that behavior left behind.

It is not easy to listen to the girls when they share about how girls or boys out in the world have been mean to them in one way or another. We don't like to have anyone hurt "our girls."

*Sticks and stones may break my bones,*
*but words can never harm me.*

They parrot this saying, but we all know that words do harm at times. And we don't like to hear them hurt each other, which happens on occasion, as they say critical things about each other. In spite of all of their mother's admonitions to the contrary and affirmations that she *likes* the way they are all different, they are still not grown up enough to just love and accept each other, without expecting one to be like the other. Thankfully, this doesn't happen *too* often.

[Writing *Becoming Hulda's Girls* has helped us learn this skill to a greater depth than ever before.]

JAN. 19

Q: As walls, I bet you hear some pretty juicy gossip, right?

A: There is an occasional story passed along under the guise of news, but their mother strongly discourages gossip. She is more likely to encourage empathy... "how would you feel if someone said that about you?" and the Golden Rule... "Is that what you would want someone to do unto you?" and understanding... "You don't know the whole story, so it's probably best not to pass that along."

For that reason, we don't get much juicy gossip at all.

*People who live in glass houses should never throw stones. If you can't say something nice, don't say anything at all.*

## JAN. 20
Q: Tell one of the most gruesome stories with lasting results that you heard.

A: Having grown restless with a dinner outing that lasted too long, (Their father was a notoriously slow eater.) Linda and Sharon were excused to go outside to play. With very few options available, they were drawn to the large painted rocks that were part of the landscaping in front of the family's favorite restaurant, the Indian Acres. After successfully leaping from rock to rock down the whole line, Sharon dared Linda to do the same, claiming with great confidence that she *probably couldn't.* Who could resist such a dare? Apparently Sharon was right, for it wasn't long before Linda slipped and fell, smashing her mouth right into a rock. Back into the restaurant they went, blood, tears and all. Beside the pain, Linda was crushed, for even before the bleeding was stopped, they could see that, sure enough, the teeth were chipped, her brand new front teeth! Mom was concerned that Sharon had pushed Linda down, but Linda was quick to admit that she had just fallen all on her own. Her patent leather shoes were still pretty slick on the bottom, and she just wasn't up to the challenge. She often tried to do the kind of physical feats that Sharon was capable of, but more often than not, she was met with defeat. Poor thing. She just had to find her *own* way of being successful.

[Linda's smile contained a gaping hole all the way through college, and braces did not straighten her crooked teeth until she was 65...delayed gratification at its best!]

### JAN. 21

**Q.** Other than playing outdoors, do the girls do anything special to get or stay in shape?

A: Marilyn, who needs it most, is not interested.

Sharon is so athletic, dancing, climbing trees, playing baseball, and such, that she has no need.

Linda and Marcia, though, do exercises on the living room floor, watching Paul Fogarty on the TV. At such times, their mother reminds them of the days when she was a young school teacher, and she and her housemates would do upside down bicycling and roll all around the floor like a ball, holding their ankles. Somewhere along the way, she gave up such activities, and has become a bit overweight. The girls tease her mercilessly about her tummy. " What tummy?" she says, sucking it in. "Why I used to model for Roland's Department Store, and didn't even need to wear a girdle like the other girls." Those were the days!

[Mom's roommate Janey Holman was a physical education teacher and fitness nut. She inspired all the others. We have maintained  life-long habits of exercise to one degree or another.]

**JAN. 22**

Q: Was there a scene that particularly touched your hearts?

A: Usually the girls' parents resolve conflict in quiet ways, between the two of them. Their mom avoids conflict almost at all costs. She tolerates her husband's tendency to drink too much, and lets him alone when he is in such a state, but one terrible night he was belligerent and loud, not his usual acquiescent self. This frightened little Linnie terribly. With Linnie in tears, Sharry, just two years older and frightened herself, wrapped her arms around her little sister, and held on tight. Two little frightened girls kneeling on the bed together, holding onto each other for dear life. Soon it was over, and, thankfully, it never happened again.

**JAN. 23**

Q: Is there anything that tickles you walls, something that fascinates you?

A: With light from a flashlight, the twins sometimes entertain the little ones by making shadow figures on the wall. A barking dog, a bunny with floppy ears, and a flying bird are favorites. Are there others?

**JAN. 24**

Q: "Mirror, Mirror on the wall. Who's the Fairest of them all?" We know you walls have no mirror on you in the bedroom, but do you have any ideas about these fair girls?

A: What's true of their mother is that she thinks each one is beautiful in her own way. Following that lead, we will point out what we see.

Marilyn is well liked because she is so warm and accepting of everyone, a real peacemaker. She has the most beautiful green eyes like her mother, a rare genetic trait, and a warm smile with straight teeth and full lips. She also has soft expressive hands, nicely shaped nails with large half moons at the cuticles, and soft, naturally wavy almost black hair.

Marcia is thin and strong physically. She has big brown eyes to go with her medium brown hair that she loves to fashion in creative ways. With a ready sense of humor and a happy-go-lucky smile, her face is lit up with excitement and appreciation most of the time.

Sharon has naturally curly strawberry blonde/red hair that is usually in banana curls. Need we say more? She also has straight teeth, a captivating smile, a quick wit, and an athletic, very coordinated body.

Linda has almost straight dishwater blonde hair, large green eyes, dimples, a nice straight nose, and a thin little body. Her amiable ways make up for many areas where she lacks. Fortunately, she has a knack for fixing her hair, and all sorts of other things as well. If anything in the house goes on the "fritz", she is the one to fix it.

*Beauty is only skin deep.*

**JAN. 25**

Q: What happens when the girls are sick?

A: When they are sick, the girls have to stay home alone all day, which is boring and lonely, so they gen-

erally go on to school if at all possible. Their teacher
mom doesn't miss school for any reason. They get some
pretty special treatment, though, including a meal
served on a tray in bed consisting of a three-minute
egg served on a little milk glass chick with dry strips
of toast to dip into the egg, and a cup of tea. It is a
time for reading stories, catching up on sleep, and
especially enjoying poetry.

[To this day, Linda and Marcia like three-minute
eggs, as symbols of care during times of illness.
Sharon hates them because they remind her of being
sick, and she hates being sick. Marilyn was known to
love breakfast in bed. We all love stories and poetry.]

*An apple a day keeps the doctor away.*

## JAN. 26

Q: What good traits do you see the girls developing?

A: Marcia gets tired of working so hard on her homework, but she is developing perseverance that may
serve her well in the years ahead. She loves to please
her dad, and is always well groomed. She is becoming
a very nurturing person; she'll probably always be
teaching, no matter what she ends up doing.

Marilyn knows what she wants and goes about getting
it. She's not afraid to work hard for what she wants.
She is a natural leader.

Sharon has energy to burn. If she gets it going in the
right direction, there will be no stopping her. Her good
mind will serve her well.

Linda has been a bit shy as a youngster, but she is developing a neat love for people. She has a heart of compassion, and an eye for beauty. Her soft-spoken ways just might have a power of their own.

### JAN. 27

Q: In spite of the good, do you see any potential character flaws developing that disturb you?

A:   Marcia - She can be flighty, frivolous, lacking in self-motivation, unable to get beyond the inertia of where she is, might miss the forest for the trees.

Marilyn - She can be controlling; she is a leader who sometimes goes too far. Still, she doesn't always have her own urges under control, like in eating.

Sharon - Her strong will can really get her into trouble at times leading to self-defeating behavior. She can be stubborn and egotistical, and discouraged by the smallest hint of failure.

Linda - She can be very self-centered, living in her own world, lacking in the ability or will to stand up for herself, even in a conversation.

[For a fun comparison of the girls' personality traits, see Appendix E]

### JAN. 28

Q: What is the most miraculous thing you have seen the girls do?

A: All four living together daily in such a small amount of space and not killing each other. In fact, most often they are very loyal and fond of one another. They often cry for one another's joys and pain, and defend each other. You don't want to mess with a Gotch Girl if one of her sisters is around.

**JAN. 29**
Q: From conversations you overhear, what are the girls dreaming about?

A: Marcia and Marilyn seem to admire their Mom's life as a teacher. They talk of going to the very same college she went to in order to follow in her footsteps, learning to be teachers.

As a youngster, Sharry talked of little else besides dancing and drumming. Mom inspired her to be a teacher, and since having Miss Hoyle, her P.E. teacher in junior high, she's thinking physical education is what she would like to teach.

After Linda's stay in the hospital with an eye infection at the age of five, the only thing she seems to dream about is being a nurse.

Encouraged by the romantic tunes of the day, most of the girls dream of falling in love and marrying a tall, dark, and handsome man like their dad. They dream of being "all grown up", of being strong, competent women, like their mother, and of having girls of their own.

Sharon is the exception; she would prefer to never grow up. She wants to be a kid forever.

**JAN. 30**
Q: What are some of the values and expectations Hulda has for her girls?

A:  1) Be grateful for each day. Enjoy it. Look for the good in every situation and every person.

2) With integrity and honesty, be confidant and humble about who you are.

3) You have work to do; don't be afraid to work hard to accomplish your goal.

4) Keep learning and growing. Be patient with the process.

5) Pick good friends. Be loyal to them and to your family.

6) Resolve your conflicts. Learn to forgive. Let bygones be bygones.

*Two wrongs don't make a right.*

7) Be respectful in your words, not swearing or using foul language.

8) Try to be loving, not hateful, in all that you do.

9) Don't be a slave to earthly goods. They come and go, but take care of what you have.

10) Stay away from unhealthy habits like smoking, drinking alcohol, and drugs. Your life is too precious to waste.

JAN. 31

Q: You've seen it all, haven't you?

A: Yes, we saw the immense delight when the little premature twins were finally able to come home from the hospital, and watched over their little cribs. We saw them grow into toddlers and witnessed their little tea parties with Petey and Baumin, their imaginary friends. We saw a tired but happy new mother getting through the Great Depression with two extra mouths to feed, sewing them clothes until two in the morning. We saw that same mother get sick in her pregnancy five years later, but survive to delight in her little red-haired daughter, with ringlets as red as her grandfather's beard. We watched over her crib, too, and saw the excitement of the twins at having a little sister. We saw the fear on the mother's face just two years later when she was expecting again, and saw that fear relieved by a normal pregnancy and delivery, a fourth girl. Again, we watched over that little crib. There was certainly disappointment for the dad, but not for that mother. She *loved* her girls! As the bedroom walls, we are so glad she was a girl. If she had been a boy, they probably would have had to move to a bigger house. This way we were able see all the other years go by as those little birds grew up and flew away. And we saw the strong contented matron of the family, the widow in her waning years, come into this room and just sit for a bit, remembering, and thanking the Lord for her greatest blessing, those four girls.

*Hildegard*

*Our Bedroom*

Now I lay me down
to sleep,
I pray thee, Lord,
my soul to keep;
If I should die be-
fore I wake
I pray thee, Lord,
my soul to take.

*Linda w/Friskie*

Marcia

Marilyn

Sharon

Linda

## *Be Mine or Be Ours*

**FEB. 1**

February, the month of love. Love begins at home, with our family, with the love between Mom and Dad. Though they don't show a lot of affection toward each other, we never question their rock solid love. They quietly, without complaint, serve one another. "I'll have my coffee now," Frank says, and Hulda willingly sets it before him. Whether he likes it or not, day after day, year after year, six days a week, Dad gets up and goes to work to provide for his family. Mom works at school all week, and does all the rest on weekends. "There's no rest for the wicked," she facetiously says.

*There's no rest for the wicked.*

**FEB. 2**

We know also that there *was* a great deal of romance in their nine years of courting. We have seen the pictures; we have heard the stories. They sometimes make us blush and giggle, but we love it, too. Mom was so beautiful; Dad was so handsome! Nine years of courtship? Why so long? Well, it was the Great Depression, no one had money, and everyone thought they should wait. Finally Hulda said, "Marry me or I'm going to move away and start over in another community." Fortunately for us, Frank decided to go with his sweetheart's plan instead of everyone else's.

**FEB. 3**

They were married, the Great Depression continued, the twins were born, and everyone survived. They rented a house across the street and two doors down from the Big House. Mom made all of the clothes for the twins until they were five years old, sometimes by refashioning clothes from Aunt Millie and Aunt Tillie, for it was impossible to buy material during the depression. Even during a depression, though, if your refrigerator poops out, you get it fixed or find a way to buy a new one, so the Gotch Radio was a viable business.

**FEB. 4**

After the Depression, came World War II. Uncle Johnny and Uncle Jerry went off to war to serve their country. Frank stayed home to mind the store, which now supported his wife and three children, for Sharon had been added in 1943. People were reluctant to spend money on live entertainment, but would purchase records as a thrifty alternative, so the store continued to prosper.

**FEB. 5**

The war ended. Linda was born in 1946. Few
memories were recorded in photos as the camera was
broken, and Uncle Jerry, the family photographer, was
not around. Though there is not much of a record of it,
we know everyone grew to school age.

**FEB. 6**

At the Gotch Radio, red foil hearts now hang from
the low ceiling of the record shop, and little fat cupids
with their bows and arrows line the walls. The
crooner's love songs are all the go: *All the Things You
Are* (Frank Sinatra), *It Had to Be You* (Bing Crosby),
*Moon River* (Andy Williams), and *Love Letters in the
Sand* (Pat Boone). Love Love Love. The individual
listening booths at the back of the record department
are especially busy this time of year, particularly
with young lovers wanting to be alone. Dad provides
appropriate supervision, lest it become the "Gotch
Radio Petting Zoo."

**FEB. 7**

The window of Hill Brothers Confectionary on
Main Street is full of big red heart-shaped boxes
of candy and yellow Whitman Sampler boxes. We
dream of a day when a real sweetheart might buy us
such an extravagant gift. In our plain candy boxes,
the chocolate covered nuts get eaten first, and the
caramels. Coconut and chocolate creams come next,
or a mint if there is one. Only as a last resort, are
all of the other creams eaten. They all have holes
punched in the bottom. Someone has been searching
for the least offensive one. No one ever admits to this
clandestine activity; we all do it in secret.

## FEB. 8

Making our own valentines is not easy, but it's fun. Cutting out red construction paper hearts is harder than it looks. Folding the paper in half is easy but then you have to draw and cut out half a heart. After you draw it, you look at it and it looks ok, but then when you cut it out you see that it is way too fat on top or way too skinny and looks scrawny. If it's too fat you can trim it down, but the skinny one just has to be thrown away unless you need a couple of smaller hearts for decoration.

To make a nice sturdy valentine, sometimes you want to cut two hearts, exactly the same, and glue them together, with some doily edging glued in between. Getting two exactly the same is the problem. It's hard to cut through four thicknesses of paper. The big girls have to help with this, as little fingers are just not strong enough. A few store bought valentines are available, but homemade are definitely preferable. They show that you care enough to put your own time and effort into it.

## FEB. 9

Marcia takes her time, and makes sure each valentine is just the way she wants it, unique to each person she has in mind. She ponders the right wording, imagining out loud the response it will get. With this involved process, she is only able to make a few. Marilyn has no time for such detail; her goal is speed and efficiency. If it is a little lopsided or a little too fat or thin, that doesn't seem to bother her; she has other things to do. Sharon's hearts are nearly perfect, but still not up to her ideal standard. And Linda ends up with valentines *full* of the smaller variety, creatively arranged, of course, and with thoughtful wording.

## FEB. 10

Almost every valentine, note, or card we ever receive has these letters at the bottom: OX. OX? What do oxen have to do with love? Of course we learned early on that it was all a secret code. O's for hugs, and X's for kisses. Pass it on. OX

[Historical tidbit: In the Middle Ages, when many people were unable to read or write, documents were often signed using an X. Kissing the X represented an oath to fulfill obligations specified in the document. The X and the kiss eventually became synonymous.]

## FEB. 11

We might write an X at the bottom of our valentines, but since we are little, we never want our valentines to actually *kiss* us. That would be way too mushy. It would make you want to barf!

[We look forward to that, though, when we are much older.]

## FEB. 12

Since it is President Lincoln's birthday, it is a day to concentrate on our love for our country, and our inspiring leaders, George Washington and Abraham Lincoln, whose portraits hang in our schoolrooms all year round. Today we did the art project of cutting out silhouettes of the two of them in black construction paper, as we do every year. It's pretty tricky business.

You know how to tell which is which, of course. Lincoln has that big stovepipe hat, and Washington has a little ponytail at the bottom of his wig.

**FEB. 13**

In preparation for the Valentine's Day parties, on every teacher's desk is a big Valentine box with a slot at the top. Mom always lets us decorate hers at home in the weeks before Valentine's Day. Teachers receive the biggest, most flowery valentines. Past, present and future students all want to prove their *love* for Mrs. Gotch, so her Valentine box is packed by the end of the day.

Here is a sample:

DEAR TEACHER
*I'll be as good as I can be;*

*I'll study hard, and behave just fine.*

*And just to prove I'm fond of you,*

*I'm sending you this Valentine.*

The most common verse of all:
*Roses are red,        Violets are blue,*
*Sugar is sweet,        And so are you.*

**FEB. 14**

Valentines' Day at school is an exciting event. Each desk has a paper lunch sack attached to the side, uniquely decorated with hearts, of course, some quite simple and others elaborate, personal mailboxes, waiting for all of the anticipated valentines. Refreshments are served, fancy cupcakes to go with our little bottles of milk. At the end, the milk monitor for the day collects all of the bottles into the metal basket, and we all go home with our hearts and tummies full, and paper sacks bulging.

**FEB. 15**

Every valentine message is analyzed at home as to what it means. Does so and so *really* like you or just like you? Did he give that kind of valentine to everyone, or just to *you*? Does this girl want to be friends or *best* friends? Which valentines are the prettiest and most creative? What if the boy you really *don't* like gives you a mushy valentine? You just have to throw it away from you with a shriek, as if it has cooties. (That's not very nice!) Many of the valentines include candy conversation hearts with their cryptic messages...   BE MINE   LOVE YOU KISS ME.   All that has to be decoded as to what it means or what we hope it means.

**FEB. 16**

Part of the post-valentine fun is Mom's sharing her valentines with us. We go over them one by one, sometimes laughing at the funny rhymes the children have made up. "Roses are red, Violets are blue, You have a face like a B22." Do you suppose a *boy* made that one up?

**FEB. 17**

Aunt Millie's candy tin, stashed under the record counter, holds a different kind of candy each month.*

This month it's cherry-flavored jelly red hearts the size of a fat quarter. Another dish holds cinnamon redhots. How we love those special treats! They help us get through the long afternoons.

*See Appendix F

**FEB. 18**

Mom gives out many loving hugs. Marcia expands them into great bear hugs. Marilyn's hugs are more polite, but she always wants a quick kiss on the lips. Sharon backs away when the hugs are being given, and Linda lavishes in them, never seeming to get enough, but not kisses on the lips! Though we do not receive a great deal of input from Dad, he can be counted on to give us an encouraging hug around the shoulders, a hug of encouragement or congratulations, when the time is right.

**FEB. 19**

Mom and Dad's love was the beginning; we are the continuation. Mom never lets us forget about the importance of sisterly love, often reminding the older sisters to look after the younger two. "Hold the little ones' hands," she says. Marcia generally takes Sharon's hand, and Marilyn takes responsibility for the baby, which is a great trial at times for babies tend to be much too slow, though she is moving as fast as her little legs can go. "And stick together in a crowd," Mom warns.

*A sister is a friend for life.*

**FEB. 20**

For us, "Be Mine" is almost always "Be *Ours.*" It is *our* crayons, *our* paper, *our* dolls, *our* games, *our* turn, *our* mess, *our* room, *our* home, *our* neighbors, *our* car, *our* church, *our* school, *our* friends, *our* business, *our* town, and *our* country.

**FEB. 21**

The love and loyalty we enjoy at home spreads outward, as we are encouraged to develop friendships. Being twins, Marcia and Marilyn have shared friends, but they each have separate friends as well. Sharon prefers the friendship of boys since she is a tomboy and they like to do the kinds of things she likes to do. Linnie, being shy, spends much time with her doll, paper doll, and stuffed animal friends. Her school friends are quiet, too, full of secrets and giggles.

**FEB. 22**

Growing up, we are taught to love God and fear hell. We go to church every Sunday and every other holy day. During Lent, we sometimes go to mass and communion every single day. We try to remember to say our prayers at night before we go to sleep, and always say grace before our Sunday dinner. We go to catechism on Saturdays and learn our lessons. Only Dad is excused. He gets to stay home and listen to the evangelists on the radio. We get to pray for his soul.

*Be sure to practice what you preach.*

**FEB. 23**

By now, in the record department, it is down

with the cupids and up with the shamrocks and leprechauns with St. Patrick's Day just a few weeks away. Our cousins, the Ahearns are Irish Catholics as are many of our friends in the community. Aunt Millie does a great job of keeping the store looking festive and fun.

**FEB. 24**

For most of us, this month is filled with sweets, but Mom doesn't care much for sweets; she likes salty things better. That's probably another reason why she has high blood pressure. She always says that if she had a quart of ice cream in the freezer, and it was up to her, it would last a month or more, but a can of peanuts would be gone in no time. She and Dad are particularly fond of cashews, as well.

**FEB. 25**

We don't put the teeth we lose under our pillow for the tooth fairy to find like many other children do. With so many of us in our beds, maybe that would get confusing. Instead, we put our tooth in a little jelly glass of water on the kitchen windowsill. In the morning, we always find coins in the water. Apparently the tooth fairy doesn't care if it is under your pillow or in a glass on the windowsill.

**FEB. 26**

At our house, we have been encouraged to always eat everything on our plate. It's called belonging to the "Clean Plate Club." After all, children are starving in other parts of the world. How cleaning our plate will help those starving children, we do not know. We all love to eat, and have good appetites anyway.

[Now that we are older and have had to struggle with our weight, we want to withdraw our membership from the "Clean Plate Club."]

*Waste not, want not.*

**FEB. 27**

Even better than the food for our bodies, is the food for our minds and hearts. Our menu consists of tons of imaginative play, zillions of books, stacks of records, choral performances (Marilyn), saxophone (Marcia), drum (Sharon), and piano lessons (Linda), frequent band concerts, and a scattering of cultural and historical events. Because of Mom's love for theatre, we love drama as well, often working backstage or acting in plays.

**FEB. 28**

*"I'll be loving you, always,"* the song says, and Mom does. Hers is a lifetime commitment, and a never-ending romance, in spite of trials and pitfalls, disease and disappointment.

[On August 16, 1965, the day our father died, her journal entry reads simply "Today my darling died."]

# My Thoughts on Love

*Love*

*Love*

*Love*

Gotch Grandparents

Greeneberg Grandparents

Mom and Aunt Martha

*Love*

*Love*

*Love*

Sisters Still Having Fun Together

# Chapter Seven      Any March
## *Did He Really Break Even?*

**MARCH 1**

"In like a lamb, out like a lion" … Mom has these words ready today for her bulletin board at school. It means if March starts out with nice warm spring-like weather, it will surely end in a blustery winter day. But there is more to the saying. "In like a lion, out like a lamb." If it starts out wintry, it will surely be spring by the end. Looks like it will be spring in the end, as usual. We have to continue our hibernation a little longer.


**MARCH 2**

Linda is always happy about March no matter what the weather. It's her birthday month. She's counting the days, quietly humming "Happy Birthday to me" as she is piddling around with her various little activities.

## MARCH 3

Dad came home today whistling *When Irish Eyes Are Smiling*. He always whistles when he's happy. He had put out the Irish records at the store in hopes that a few Irish folks would come to buy them. "Everyone is Irish this time of year," he says. He was in such a good mood. Uncle Russell probably came by the store to share a few Irish jokes with him. He is the one person that can really get Dad to laugh.

[Dad also enjoyed the humor of Jimmy Durante, Victor Borge, and Red Skelton, and was known to imitate Louis Armstrong blowing his horn in a very entertaining way.]

## MARCH 4

Mom needed more shamrocks for her room at school, so she got out the stencils of manila tag board, and we went to work. We all love to work on projects like this. Since we had the kitchen table all a mess anyway, we decided to make some nice juicy pictures with the finger paints, which we did. Then we really had a mess, so we had to clean up, especially Dad's place at the table. Other than their bedroom, it's really the only space that is *his* and he likes it usable. He's so tolerant of all our stuff everywhere, but just imagine, the poor guy has to live with *five* messy creative females!

## MARCH 5

Linda is getting more excited each day about having her birthday, usually just a quiet affair with the family, but Mom will fix her favorite dinner of country spare ribs cooked in a barbecue sauce made of A1

sauce and catsup, baked potato, and lima beans. She
loves baby lima beans! Of course Mom will bake her a
cake, too.

## MARCH 6

Linda never tires of hearing the story of her "birth
day" which Mom tells with great joy. It was such a
beautiful spring morning that she put Sharry in the
stroller and took her for a walk to town. Mr. Powers,
from across the street, was out working in his yard,
planting grass seed here and there. Indeed, *everyone*
seemed to be outdoors enjoying the weather. After
they arrived back home, Mom went into labor.  Being
born on a beautiful day makes you feel like the whole
world is celebrating your birth.  At four pounds, three
ounces, Linda was the largest baby of the four, all of
us having been born at seven months.  The twins were
so tiny they had to be in incubators for a while.

## MARCH 7  LINDA'S BIRTHDAY.

Today is Linda's most special birthday, the one when
she turns seven…seven on the seventh.  Six girls from
school are invited for a party, so that, including Linda, the number at the party will be seven. The party
includes playing pin the tail on the donkey, opening
presents, and eating cake and ice cream. Throughout
the party, Linda looks for Glenda, her colored friend,
but Glenda never comes. This is heartbreaking, a
great mystery to her, a big disappointment. Did she
forget? Was she not able to afford a present, and didn't
want to come without one? Did her parents think it
wasn't safe because of her being colored? [ How can
seven year olds understand the complexity of issues
regarding race in the year 1953?]

## MARCH 8

Linda is a year older, but will always remain "the baby." Now that she is in school, the extreme shyness she suffered during the preschool years is gradually being replaced with greater confidence and enjoyment of people. She is a good student, but is easily distracted from serious work by opportunities to do something fun. In our house, the opportunities come frequently. Someone always wants to play checkers, kept conveniently slid under the couch, or Cootie, or Pit, or Monopoly, or card games of all kinds. Our folks play Canasta with Spoof (Ralph) and Eleanor Hart every Saturday night, so we learned the complicated rules to that game when we were quite young, but we also enjoy Rummy and Hearts, as well as Kings in the Corner. To ever win one of these games, Linda has to play with Mom, for the older girls are merciless, and reluctant to ever share strategies for winning.

[The twins were especially fond of bridge, and spent many hours playing that, especially when they were in college.]

## MARCH 9

While our kitchen table, with it's cozy breakfast nook, is the hub of activity of all kinds, supper itself is restrictively quiet. The daily paper comes shortly before Dad arrives home from work, and he insists on reading it during the evening meal. This is so difficult for us! After a full day at school, we have so much to talk about, but we can't. Our saving grace is that we know immediately after dinner, Dad will retire early to bed. After that, we can chat to our heart's content.

[This rather strange behavior, which we accepted as normal, was explained by the fact that he had "sugar diabetes." It may have been simply his way of escaping from five talkative women. He was generally a quiet person himself.]

## MARCH 10

With Dad gone, the breakfast nook comes alive with chatter. Of course we share the activities of the day and who said what to whom with the resulting consequences, but we also air our frustrations, share our hopes and dreams, express our fears, argue about life's truths and make plans for the future. Sharon and Marcia are the great popcorn makers, shaking the heavy lidded pot on the stove to keep the popcorn from burning, drizzling it with real melted butter, and adding lots of salt. Or sometimes we make a batch of cookies and heat up a pan of milk on the stove to make cocoa. The smells of these comfort foods and the laughs and tears get all mixed together around our good old breakfast nook.

## MARCH 11

Sometimes Dad escapes to the Elk's Club on Friday nights to play cards. He likes to play poker, and they play for money. "How'd you do?" we ask to see if he won or not.

"I broke even," he always says. Mom says she isn't sure about that, but if he loses, he doesn't lose much. These days we don't have that much to lose. Sometimes, if we are asking Dad for money to do something, and it is the next day after his breaking even, he breaks out a wad of bills from his pocket to share some with us. On these days, he will often give us a few extra dollars. We wonder, "Did he really break even?"

## MARCH 12

Mom had a meeting after school today, so the twins helped the little ones get their homework done, and then we all played board games. Marilyn won every game, as usual. Marcia just laughed; she loves to play games no matter who wins. Linda quit early and switched to coloring for awhile. Sharon hung in there, but got very upset when it became obvious she was not going to win. Marcia tried to comfort her, "Remember, it's not whether you win or lose but how you play the game that counts." Sharon disagreed; she hates to lose, period!

## MARCH 13

Today, Sharry avoided the twins; she was still sensitive about her loss. She and Linda played Sorry. Sharon started cheating. Linda tried harder. Sharry took advantage. Linda was flustered, and close to tears. Sharry quit competing, and helped Linda by sharing some obvious strategy. Linda felt victorious. Sharry felt joy. Maybe it *is* about how you play the game.

*When you cheat, you only hurt yourself.*

## MARCH 14

After church today, instead of the beef and pork roast that we usually have, we had corned beef, cabbage, and potatoes, in honor of St. Patrick's Day, which is this week. We sat at the dining room table, and Mom had put the pretty tablecloth on with the violets for spring. We used the good white dishes and our best table manners. No one belched out loud, we used napkins instead of wiping our mouth on the nearest dishtowel, we chewed with our mouths closed, and we didn't talk with food in our mouths. Dad didn't even read the paper. He had already read the *Sunday Tribune* while we were at church. It was almost like being at Aunt Martha's.

## MARCH 15

We all take Latin as our foreign language in high school. During these years, we celebrate the Ides of March on this day. We pretend to be Roman citizens dressed in togas made out of sheets, or Roman slaves dressed in gunnysacks. We eat sitting on the floor, and make our slaves peel the grapes for us, or we are the slaves peeling the grapes. We eat greasy roast pig, which is pretty gross looking and smelling, and wish each other "Bona Fortuna" all around.

## MARCH 16

Another celebration we have heard about this month is Mardi gras. We never celebrate Mardi gras in our town as far as I know. We don't have a St. Patrick's Day parade, either, like the big one they have in Chicago, which we sometimes see on the news. On Ash Wednesday, we go to church and get ashes on our forehead as a sign of our sorrow over our sin or something. We wear them rather proudly. I guess you could say that we are proud to be humble. Most of the other kids are Catholic, too, so they have ashes on their foreheads, too, so we don't seem too weird. We never give too much thought to what we are going to give up for Lent. We always give up candy, especially chocolate. We love chocolate!

## MARCH 17

St. Patrick's Day at school was fun this year. Someone in the twins' room brought in homemade Irish soda bread for an after-recess snack. Sharon and Linda had shamrock sugar cookies. Mom's class had cupcakes with shamrocks on the top. Mom brought the extra ones home for us. That was the "luck of the Irish" part. The *unlucky* part was that Dad didn't come home for supper. That always makes Mom nervous; she worries about his safety. She didn't say anything, but we knew. We didn't say anything either, but we were worried, too. We knew he'd probably come home "tight," as Mom called it sometimes. He still wasn't home when we went to bed. He was out celebrating St. Patrick's Day in his own way.

## MARCH 18

First thing in the morning, we checked the big chair in the living room to see if Dad's long pants were there. That's where he always puts them if he comes in late. His pants were there. Thank goodness!! He slept in a little today. He must have come in pretty late. When he got up, he was extra sweet. Mom says he's a different man when he isn't drinking. We agree.

It happens to be Uncle Johnny's birthday today. We gave him a card. He was surprised. We have no idea how old he is. Since he lives all alone in the Big House, it must be kind of lonely. We should trade places with him. Our little house would be perfect for one guy and that big old Victorian would be lovely for all of us. We always say that, but it would never happen, and we know that. We love our little home anyway; we wouldn't really want to trade.

## MARCH 19    DAD'S BIRTHDAY

We always give Dad clothes for his birthday. We all love to see him at his handsome best. This year, we gave him a striking corduroy sport coat with brown and black stripes. He looks so sharp in that! He'll have his birthday cake with no frosting because of his diabetes, but for a special treat he may eat it first, before the meal. We love it when he does that, because then we get to do it, too. He might have it right after his beer and Limburger cheese spread on little party rye. It smells so horrible, we can smell it when we come in the front door, and we always groan, "Oh Dad. How can you eat that stuff?" but he loves it. The one exception is Marcia; she'll eat it with him. Unbelievable. Honestly, the smell alone can make you gag; it smells like toe jam!

## MARCH 20

It's beginning to be spring. The bushes are full of pussy willows. We brought some in and stuck them in a canning jar. They are so sweet and soft, like our own little kitty.

## MARCH 21

Time to walk to town and shop for our Easter outfits. This year it is navy blue cotton coats with trim white collars, white gloves, patent leather Mary Janes, white anklets and, of course, hats, that is, Easter bonnets. We love our Easter bonnets; when they are new, they are neat and fun. On the way home, we sing "In your Easter Bonnet with all the frills upon it..."

These same hats, after they get crammed into the top shelf of the closet a few times, will get all wibber-jawed, all bent out of shape, and will look stupid.

Then we will despise the fact that we have to wear them, but for now, we will just enjoy them, and look forward to how fun it will be on Easter morning, to see and be seen in all of our Easter glory.

[Our love of hats goes back as far as Mom's collection before she was married and forward as far as Sharon's collection of over three hundred.]

**MARCH 22**

Our shopping expedition was similar to those of the past. In general, we enjoy shopping. We each love something best about it. Linda likes to see her feet in the magic machine at the shoe store, where you can see your bones all green*. She has to sing the Buster Brown jingle. "Hi, I'm Buster Brown; I live in a shoe. Here's my dog Tyge; he lives there, too." Marcia's favorite is to find just the right shoes to match her outfit, so we shop for shoes last. Marilyn loves everything, but especially enjoys stopping for homemade pie at Ruth's restaurant on the way home. As the day drags on, Sharry's patience wears thin, especially the hat part. Some of her sisters are *so* indecisive!

*[This machine was banned in the 1970's.]

**MARCH 23**

Rainy weather forced us to spend a day in the basement. Mom wanted us to get down there and pitch out some of our old toys. That is a hard task for most of us, for some of our best treasures are in the basement. We love to go through all those musty old comic books, remember with fondness our little play house, finger again the baby toys, like the Hobart wooden peg board and stack of rings, and the rubber seven dwarfs. There is an old abacus down there, boxes of broken crayons, our old pencil boxes with little teeth-marked pencil stubs, and an old fancy pen that Mom had when she was a young teacher. When you flip up the lever on the side, a little tube projects from the nib, and it sucks up the ink. In a little box are the beads that made up the little bracelets that were placed on the twins' wrists in the hospital when they were born. They are little white circles that say, GOTCH, with pink beads on the sides. So many precious things!!

In the orange crates, next to the jars of pickles and green beans Mom used to can, there are puzzles we may want to put together again some day. We ran across Linda's little yellow scooter, remembering how proud she was that Mom let her paint it herself a few years ago, a big thing, since she was still so young. The roller skates are down there. Pretty soon we'll be able to go out and do that again. And pretty soon we'll get the bikes out and clean them up. Spring is such an exciting time of year!

**MARCH 24**

The buttercups are blooming out front in the morning sun, and after the rain, there is a lot of nice oozy mud, which Marilyn and Sharon love to use for making mud pies. After school, they sat on the brick wall back by the Ross' little patio and patted away. Marcia and Linda want nothing to do with mud pies.

[Marilyn loved to make real pies until the day she died. She could whip up a pie in no time, which we were all happy to consume.]

## MARCH 25

We saw so many flowers beginning to bloom on the way to school, this would have been a good day for the teacher to ask us to draw what we saw on the way to school. She didn't. Tonight we had to study for our weekly Friday spelling tests. Marilyn already knew all of her words. Marcia was busy writing hers another five times. Sharon lost her tear-off sheet, but assured Mom that she knew them. She probably did. She nearly always got an A. Linda was saying them out loud to Mom and getting them right. We love spelling.

## MARCH 26

It was quiet at the Gotch Radio today, so none of us had to work until nine the way we usually do on Friday nights. We often have to miss school events or go late because of our work hours; that is just the price we pay for being part of a family business. To celebrate, we took out one of our favorite puzzles, one depicting a huge bouquet of spring flowers, and went to work. Marilyn and Linda tired early and went on to bed. Marcia and Sharon kept on, just wanting to put in one more piece. At midnight, Mom got back up and said, "Are you girls still up? You get to bed and get your beauty sleep! Tomorrow is another day." So they did.

*Tomorrow is another day.*

## MARCH 27

Saturday mornings are hectic at our house. Dad has to deliver and pick up Sharon from her early drum lesson, rush home to pick up Marcia and head back

to town for Sharon's dance class and for Dad to open
the store by nine. Marcia accompanies Sharon during
the lessons to take notes on what the steps are to the
dances and to get any other relevant information.
Marilyn, Linda, and Mom stay home to do the weekly
housecleaning and laundry.

Catechism class is on Saturday, too, so Linda has
to try to find the catechism papers and memorize
the assignment for the week. Even thinking about it
makes her get butterflies in her stomach, for Sister
Carmen is quite stern, very intimidating for a rather
shy little girl. As soon as Marcia and Sharon return
from dance, we have a quick bite to eat, and then
hightail it to church, but frequently we are late, which
brings Sister Carmen's wrath upon us all the more.
She already doesn't like us because we don't go to the
Catholic school that is just two blocks from our house.
Because Mom is a teacher in the public schools, she
feels very strongly that that is where we should be,
too. Against much pressure, she stands her ground.
We are glad. The boys who ride their bikes home
from St. Anthony's school past our house are always
loud and say swear words. They don't seem as nice as
regular boys.

We survived catechism, the house is in order, the
clothes are clean, and the lessons have been learned.
It was another good day.

*The early bird catches the worm.*

**MARCH 28**

School for teachers' own *children* (kids are baby

goats) never begins or ends, it just *is*. Every incorrect English usage is corrected. There will be no "he *ain't* got no" in our home, nor "Me and her did such and such", but rather " He doesn't have any" and "She and I did such and such." Games in the car include arithmetic problems or quizzing us on our multiplication tables. One of our favorite games is when Mom goes through a complicated arithmetic series, and we have to guess the answer in the end. For example: 2 plus 10, minus 3, divided by 3, times 7 equals what? (21). We are challenged to think of synonyms and antonyms, or make up rhymes and samples of onomatopoeia. We are encouraged to memorize poetry and recite it. Mom loves poetry. She has several books of poetry that she enjoys and quotes from occasionally.

**MARCH 29**

Collections are good things to distract us from our impatience with the slow arrival of warm weather. Sharon spends many mornings and evenings sorting her baseball cards, memorizing the statistics. Trading season will soon be upon her, and she has to know what she is doing. Linda organizes her paper doll collection, and all of the doll clothes in their little suitcases and trunk. The twins organize their records and count the money in their depression-glass piggy banks, which is time-consuming because the only way to get the money out is to slide a knife into the little slot at the top and shake in such a way as to get the coins to line up with the knife. They do this spread-eagle on the floor in the living room, the coins flying everywhere and rolling at times under the couch.

**MARCH 30**

Today was a blustery day, perfect for flying kites.
Our neighbors, Butch and Marie, were out flying a
kite with their dad. It looked easy enough. We tried
to duplicate what they had with the materials at
hand, even tearing up an old sheet to make the tail,
but we didn't really have the right stuff, and we sure
didn't have a dad who was there to show us how. How
frustrating!

[Kite-flying remained one of those romantic ideals
that we just were never able to experience in our
growing up years.]

**MARCH 31**

We can never get through March without
thinking of Uncle Russell (Ahearn) and the State
Championship Basketball Team he coached in Hebron,
Illinois. It happened during March Madness in the
year 1952. After that year, at the Big House, we have
our own family victory celebrations. We watch the
game on a sheet hung up as a screen projected by a
seven-millimeter movie projector. We cheer and drink
and enjoy over and over the wonderful success of the
Green Giants. We are proud of his success, proud
that we are related to someone who has accomplished
something so big and famous.

Nice warm day today. March is going "out like a
lamb," so it's on to April.

[Sharon still never misses March Madness. The others
enjoy it, too, to one degree or another.]

# My March Activities

_Linda_

Sharon passes the Roman torch to Linda

Saturday Night Canasta w/ Harts

Uncle Russ' Green Giants are State Champs

# Chapter Eight                    Any April
## *On the Scraps of Our Lives*

**APRIL 1**
Your shoe's untied.
        (after they see it's not)
                April Fool!
Your zipper's down.
        (after they see it's not)
                April Fool!
Look up.
        Look down.
                Look at your thumb.
                (after they do)
        Gee, you're dumb.  April Fool!

Who knows where all that foolishness comes from?

## APRIL 2

*At the Gotch Radio*
*shamrocks are down,*
*Easter bunnies are up.*
*Eggs, too,*
*and Lilies.*
*Here and there,*
*a little umbrella.*
*"April showers*
*bring May flowers."*
*The candy tin is full*
*of jellybeans.*


## APRIL 3

*Holy Week Habits*
*Bless the palms,*
*weave into crosses.*
*Visit the stations,*
*pray for us sinners.*
*Kiss the feet,*
*pray for the dead.*
*Good Friday sadness;*
*statues covered in purple.*
*Waiting and waiting*
*for Lent to be over.*

## APRIL 4

*Coloring Easter eggs.*
*Boil the eggs,*
       *six apiece.*
*Spread the newspapers;*
       *set out cups;*
              *boil the water.*
*Plop in tablets,*
       *one per cup.*
              *Add stinky vinegar.*
*White crayon drawings,*
       *crosses and lilies,*
              *Add our names.*
*Fight over who's first.*
*Wire holders wobble,*
       *in and out,*
              *in and out.*
*Dark colors take too long!*
*Set eggs on cardboard stands;*
       *apply decals;*
              *admire our work.*
*Eggs ready to hide.*

**APRIL 5**

*Easter morning.*
*Hunt for eggs*
*Between books on the bookcase,*
*Among cushions on the couch,*
*Under the davenport,*
*Above the china cabinet,*
*Inside a shoe, next to the records,*
*In a slightly open sewing machine drawer,*
*Behind the statue of Mary,*
*Behind a picture frame on the piano,*
*All are found.*
*"Here comes Peter Cottontail,*
*hopping down the bunny trail..." we sing.*


**APRIL 6**

*No more Lent!*
*Dive into identical Easter baskets!*
*Fair is fair; all the same,*
*Same every year:*
*George's Candy Store*
*Big Solid Chocolate bunnies,*
*ears eaten before breakfast,*
*Little yellow peeps,*
*Chocolate covered marshmallow bunnies,*
*Scrumptious turtles,*
*Colored jellybeans,*
*Colored sugar eggs,*
*pink, yellow, blue and green*
*All nestled in green cellophane grass.*
*Who wants breakfast?*

## APRIL 7

*Off to church,*
*    looking like a million bucks.*
*Spiffy new outfits,*
*    stylish Easter bonnets.*
*Sparkly patent leather shoes,*
*    a sight to behold!!*
*Even Dad goes on Easter,*
*    in suit and bow tie.*
*Church is radiant*
*    all in white!*
*Easter Lily smells,*
*    chiming Easter bells.*
*Hallelujah!*

## APRIL 8

Favorite Easter Music
    fills our hearts:
        *The Easter Parade,*
            *Here Comes Peter Cottontail,*
        *Christ the Lord Is Risen Today*
*Gloria in Excelsis Deo*

**APRIL 9**

*Another Big House celebration:*
*The family gathers,*
*Easter lilies deck the bay window,*
*Easter dinner fills the table:*
*Pineapple glazed ham,*
*creamy scalloped potatoes,*
*mashed and marshmallowed sweet potatoes,*
*golden brown scalloped corn,*
*French green bean casserole,*
*Mandarin orange salad,*
*hot buttered rolls,*
*Lamb pound cake with coconut frosting.*
*Aromas make our tummies growl;*
*black olives get snitched;*
*relishes and rushka disappear.*
*Aunt Millie sprinkles the holy water,*
*and we "Commence!"*

**APRIL 10**

*Easter bonnet thoughts...*
*Marilyn hates hers.*
*(She just doesn't like hats.)*
*Marcia fidgets with hers.*
*(Does it look all right?)*
*Sharon wears hers proudly.*
*(It's too girly, but oh, well.)*
*Linda's keeps slipping.*
*(Where's the strap to hold it on?)*
*Mom's looks classy,*
*(even though it's last year's.)*

## APRIL 11

*Life is like a journey*
*Taken on a train,*
*With a pair of travelers*
*At each window pane.*
*I may sit beside you*
*All the journey through*
*Or I may sit elsewhere*
*Never knowing you.*
*But if fate should mark me*
*To sit by your side,*
*Let's be pleasant travelers;*
*It's so short a ride.*
*Hulda E. Gotch*


## APRIL 12

*Nice weather,*
*walk to town.*
*Wear clean dresses,*
*greet the neighbors,*
*Don't step on a crack*
*or break your mother's back.*
*Don't step on a fish square,*
*or you'll stink like a fish.*
*Kick stones on way up;*
*Drag feet on way back.*
*Mom walks straight and tall.*
*Everyone brings a plastic purse.*

## APRIL 13

*Rainy day strikes,*
*time to bake;*
*Mom bakes all morning.*
*Big yellow bowl,*
*full of dough*
*Mashed potatoes and flour*
*turn into plate-sized pancakes,*
*One after another,*
*stacked and buttered*
*between the round platters*
*on top of the stove.*
*Kitchen warm and steamy,*
*heavenly smells,*
*crunchy carrots and celery,*
*lunch surprise for Dad.*
*Please, one more stack?*
*Everyone loves luckshaw!\**

*[Actual Slovak spelling is "locsha", but luckshaw is
how we pronounced it.  Recipe in Appendix B]

**APRIL 14**

*Baseball's in the air;*
*pitchers off to training,*
*catchers suited up,*
*batters warmed up,*
*fans are hopeful.*
*Kids break in new gloves*
*and play catch.*
*Mom cheers on the Cubbies.*
*Dad supports the White Sox,*
*Nellie Fox and Minnie Minoso.*
*Even Linda has heard of Mickey Mantle.*

**APRIL 15**

*Time for taxes...*
*"Two things sure in life," Dad says,*
*"death and taxes."*
*For weeks and weeks,*
*Dad up at night*
*figuring, figuring, figuring,*
*pages and pages,*
*numbers, numbers, numbers,*
*sharp, pointy numbers*
*on long yellow papers.*
*One year auditors come.*
*Everyone's nervous;*
*they find nothing wrong,*
*sighs of relief.*
*They never come again.*
*Mom is proud of her smart*
*and honest*
*businessman.*

## APRIL 16

*Spring Saturday...*
*Clotheslines are up,*
    *wipe off the lines,*
        *clothespins in bag,*
            *wicker basket heavy with load.*
*Whites are bleachy,*
    *smelling of Linco.*
*Hang socks first,*
    *by the toes,*
        *hang undies and bras,*
            *hidden from the street,*
*Shirts by their tails,*
    *drippy with starch,*
        *colors together, dresses and shirts,*
*Towels hang separate,*
    *washcloths share clothespins.*
*Pants hang by waists,*
    *blue jeans stiff and scratchy.*
*Wooden clothes props*
    *push lines high,*
        *make us stretch.*
*Sheets flap in the breeze,*
    *pillowcases, too.*
*Sun feels good;*
    *clothes smell fresh,*
        *and look so nice*
            *all neatly folded.*
*End of a good day.*

APRIL 17

*Annual Hobby Show begins...*
*Collectors and hobbyists*
*show their wares.*
*Marcia's band*
*plays for entertainment.*
*The Armory*
*comes to life!*
*Row*
*upon row*
*upon row,*
*All you can imagine,*
*and more.*
*Salt and pepper shakers and matchbooks*
*from around the world,*
*Cookie jars,*
*all shapes and sizes,*
*Beer cans,*
*like none we've ever seen,*
*And Lionel trains,*
*through miniature towns*
*with tunnels and trees,*
*Dollhouses,*
*large wooden ones,*
*with every tiny curtain and rug just so.*
*(Roberta Rush's dad does this!)*
*It makes you shake your head*
*in wonder.*
*Where do they get it all?*
*And how do they find the time*
*To put it all together?*

## APRIL 18

*White snow gone,*
      *shabbiness appears.*
*Winter took its toll;*
      *everything needs work.*
*Windows dirty,*
      *cracked sidewalks worse,*
*Paint peeling from house,*
      *back stairs worn,*
*Metal trashcans dented,*
            *one lid missing...*
                  *garbage men are too rough!*
*Gardens all smashed,*
      *and moldy.*
*Hurry up, summer;*
*We'll get things back in shape.*

## APRIL 19

*Linnie plays dress-up*
      *in long black taffeta skirt,*
            *safety-pinned on,*
*Aunt Pauline's silver strappy heels,*
      *Mom's old purse*
            *full of play money,*
*Long white gloves,*
      *brown veiled hat,*
            *beautiful red lipstick.*
*Pushing a doll buggy*
      *or little grocery cart*
            *down to the Big House and back,*
                  *she parades.*
*O to be a grown up lady!*

**APRIL 20**

Another thunderstorm,
        many loud crashes!
The heavens have really opened up!
"Angels must be bowling,"
        says Grandma Gotch,
"Nothing to worry about,"
        but some do worry.
Tornado warnings keep us in,
        appliances are unplugged.
We play cards or color,
        try not to notice.
                Everyone notices.
Should we go to the basement?
        Should we hide under the bed?
Not this time.
        It passes us by.


**APRIL 21**

Sunny day...
        forget all about storms.
Friskie kitty
        loves the sun,
                naps on the bed,
                        licks himself clean.
Hour after hour,
        goes out
                and naps on the front porch.
Sleeps all day,
        prowls all night.
That's our Friskie!

## APRIL 22

We enjoy our yard again,
    on the corner
        with the big yard.
Sharry teaches tumbling tricks
    and dance moves.
We do somersaults,
    backwards and forwards,
And double somersaults,
    holding each other's ankles,
Toadstools and headstands,
    handstands and walk on our hands.
Sharry flips and splits,
    Linda flops and not-so-splits.
We play leapfrog and wheelbarrows,
    perfect cartwheels, learn tour je te's,
    and do back bends.
Sharry shines in all her glory.
Linda...well, that's another story,
But all for fun.

## APRIL 23

Big day for Marcia...
    first day to get glasses.
All had been blurry; now she can see!
Even leaves on the trees!
    Little spring green leaves!
It's beautiful!
    It's wonderful!
Excited for her, we all dance in circles
    and celebrate,
        two and two.

**APRIL 24**

*Nice warm sunny day,*
*    Aunt Tillie's day off,*
*        good day to spring clean*
*            the Big House.*
*She swishes lace curtains*
*    in the kitchen sink*
*        and stretches them,*
*            all drippy,*
*Onto the stretchers,*
*    where they sit*
*        in the sun, to dry.*
*She hums her way through the work,*
*    and may break into a bird song.*
*Linnie watches and watches,*
*    full of wonder.*

**APRIL 25**

*Saturday. No school.*
*Rainy again today,*
*    more April showers.*
*Monopoly day.*
*Linda out of money first,*
*    no problem, switches to paper dolls.*
*Marcia next,*
*    no problem, switches to trying out new hairdo.*
*Marilyn and Sharon battle it out.*
*    Marilyn gets richer and richer.*
*        Sharon gets madder and madder.*
*Game over.      Marilyn wins.*
*Sharon stews rest of the day;*
*    no consolation prizes work.*

## APRIL 26

*Sunday drive*
      *in the country...*
*Farmers out farming*
      *on big green tractors*
*Soil turned over,*
      *rich and black.*
*Seeds being planted,*
      *corn and soybeans.*
*Air stinky with manure...*
      *PU!!*
*Barns red*
      *against a blue sky.*
*"My father owns a grocery store" game,\**
      *girls get too loud;*
            *Dad puts on the Kibosh.*
*Car gets quiet;*
      *spoils our fun,*
            *sometimes.*
*Maybe we spoiled his fun.*
*Oh, well.*
*Nice change of scenery.*

\* see Appendix C

## APRIL 27

Mom writes poetry
on the back of envelopes
drawn from her purse,
In the waiting room,
in the car,
on a trip to somewhere,
Scraps of time
on scraps of paper,
making sense
of the sensations of life.
Pondering,
wondering,
fondling the moments,
Capturing them
in her heart.
Where are those scraps
of thoughts and dreams?
Now
they are written
on the scraps of our lives.

## APRIL 28

*Cold colorless world*
    *surrenders to a new palette*
        *of warmth and beauty.*
*Stark skeleton trees soften*
        *in cloaks of limey green.*
*Gray skies*
    *turn blue.*
*Corpse-like creek beds*
        *stretch clear.*
*Smashed grasses give way*
        *to tiny verdant spears.*
*Rainbow colors appear.*

## APRIL 29

*I've worked*
*And played*
*This beautiful day*
*After*
*Going to church*
*To hear*
*A wonderful*
*Inspirational*
*message*
*At a special*
*mission being*
*Held all week.*
*Thank You*
*Lord*

*For my eyes*
*My voice*
*My ears*
*My whole  body.*
*And all the*
*Extra special*
*blessings*
*Given me this*
*day. -* Hulda E. Gotch

## APRIL 30

                    *Beloved people*
          *treasured animals*    *cherished possessions*
      *favorite chair*                          *relished smells*
  *savored tastes*                                  *inside jokes*
  *secret sillies*          *Home*              *family funnies*
      *flights of fantasy*                        *common faith*
          *common cold*                      *healing wounds*
                  *warm cocoon of love*

# Poetry & Thoughts on Lent, Easter, Spring

Hats

Hats

Hats!

We

love...

hats!

## *Toward the Finish Line*

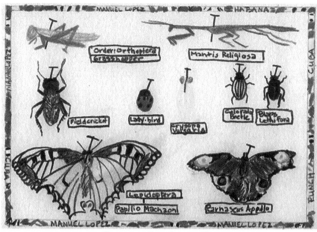

*The cigar box bug collection*

**MAY 1**

All of the little Lilies of the Valley are in full
bloom, growing by the foundation across the front, and
all down the north side of the house. We can really
make neat bouquets. Sometimes the little wood violets
that are all over the yard bloom at the same time,
which is perfect for our May baskets that we deliver
today to our neighbors. We slide the handle over the
doorknob, ring the doorbell, and run away. Sometimes
we hide in the bushes to see and hear their delight
over receiving our little surprise.

**MAY 2**

Our neighbor-girl Janey stopped by to thank us for
the lovely May basket we brought over. "When can I
help make the May baskets, Aunt Hulda?" she asked
our mom. Mom isn't really her aunt; we're not blood
relatives, but we live so close, we might as well be.
She's like our little sister or cousin.

"Pretty soon you'll be able to do it," Mom replied. Mom always makes it seem like good things are just about to happen.

## MAY 3

When Mom was a little girl in Bloomington, they used to have a big May Day celebration, where they dressed all up in their party dresses and danced around a May pole. This whole idea has always been a mystery to us until this year when Linda's class did it at school. Each person held a ribbon that was attached to the top of the pole. As the boys walked around the pole in one direction and the girls walked around the other way, going over and then under, over and then under, the ribbons wove their way down the pole. Quite magical!

## MAY 4

Since this is our last month of school, we are all getting a little antsy. Some of the afternoons are pretty hot now, and even though we open the windows to get a little fresh air, we still get pretty drowsy in the heat. Children who live on farms are needed to work in the fields during summer, so our school always ends by the first week of June. We're already starting to do some of the end of the school tests.

## MAY 5

Mom is sewing every evening now, working on Sharry's costumes for the ballet. Most of the outfits are covered with sequins and each sequin has to be sewn on individually, by hand. It's good that Mom is a good seamstress. The ballet isn't until some time next month, but she never likes to rush and do things like that in a hurry. She says it's always better to take your time and do it right. She'll just work an hour or two every night until it's done.

*Take your time, and do it right. Anything worth doing is worth doing right.*

## MAY 6

Sharry's costumes are going to be so neat! For acrobat, she's going to be a little bunny with a fuzzy white tail. Mom finished that costume tonight. Mom said that it was the easiest one, but it is darling. The other costume is lime green and fuchsia with many, many sequins. It's going to be a real labor of love.

[These costumes were so well made that they were passed down to the grandchildren and still survive, somewhere in the family.]

## MAY 7

With all of the work on costumes, we girls were inspired to play ballet, so we got out the old costumes and danced around the living room. Linda can't really do the fancy moves, but she likes to pretend anyway. She can hold her hands in the graceful way that ballerinas do. She might have liked to be a ballerina, but Rosalind Hupp's dance studio is a scary place for her. Miss Hupp seems so harsh with her hair slicked back in a steel gray bun, her muscular body, and her voice so loud and demanding. The girls are loud also, especially when they move as a herd in their tap shoes.

The place smells of sweaty bodies and rubber mats mixed with the smell of popcorn that wafts up from the movie theatre downstairs, quite nauseating. If Linnie is ever dragged to the studio for some reason, it is with fear and trembling that she watches in silence, scarcely breathing until she is back down that ominous staircase.

## MAY 8

Sharry loves her dance lessons. She adores Miss Hupp with her strength and high expectations, her no nonsense attitude. Miss Hupp is someone she can really respect! She loves the discipline, the hard work she is required to do, and the perfection demanded of her. She loves the experience of getting her body to move to the intricate rhythms, and the friendly Glen Karr who plays the piano for them. Even the smells don't bother her, for they are just a result of people working hard, which is a good thing. Sharry can do all of the positions and steps just right. She is the best tap dancer and acrobat of all; that's what we think, anyway. We're all very proud of her. She has all of the routines memorized already, and the performance is still a long ways away.

[Sharon took tap lessons and performed in recitals well into her sixties.]

## MAY 9

The spelling books are getting funny to hold with their half sheet practice sheets torn out, what with it being near the end of the year, and all. The spelling words are all really hard now, which is neat. Being able to spell difficult words is all the more satisfying than easy ones. "You are either a good speller or not," Mom says. "Either way, you still need to study your spelling." It's one of the basics, like penmanship, and if you work at it steadily, you can get it.

*Practice makes perfect.*

**MAY 10**

"It's May, It's May, the lusty month of May..." we sing, from Camelot. That has all of us thinking about romance and marriage, since June is right around the corner, the time for June brides.

- Marcia wants someone romantic and musical, like Elvis Presley.

-Marilyn wants someone smart who will earn a good living.

-Sharon wants someone like Matty, our neighbor, who is gentle, and adores her.

-And Linda wants a guy with potential, and someone who can fix things, unlike her father who can't fix anything.

We imagine ourselves to be the most beautiful brides some day, and dream of who our husbands might be. Will they be tall, dark, and handsome like our father? [Probably not! What do you think?]

**MAY 11**

After all of the talk about weddings yesterday, Linda checked the Big House wedding veil Spirea bushes, and was happy to see that they were blooming. With someone's old communion dress, old lace curtains for a veil, the white Spirea flowers for a bouquet, and a circle of mock orange sprays from out of the back yard, she was a beautiful little bride. Too bad she couldn't talk Butch, the little boy next door, into playing groom. He is her little boyfriend, but that is asking a little too much. So today she went up and down the sidewalk by herself, a wonderful little procession of one. Sharon was off playing marbles, beating the pants off the boys. The twins were gone, too, and Mom was busy cleaning. It's good the "baby" can amuse herself so well.

## MAY 12     MOTHER'S DAY

*M is for the many things she gave me.*
*O is only that she's growing old.*
*T is for the tears she shed to save me.*
*H is for her heart of purest gold.*
*E is for her eyes with love-light shining.*
*R means right and right she'll always be.*
*Put them all together they spell MOTHER, a word that*
*means the world to me.*

    This is the song we will sing to Mom on Mother's Day, this year and every year.

    Our mother was a woman of strength, wisdom, and conviction. With faith, dignity, and compassion, she moved past her fears and disappointments to do good all the days of her life.

**MAY 13**

> *My Mother*
> by Linda Gotch Helmich    May, 1980
> *My mother was a lady of the finest fashion known.*
> *She kept us all together;*
>> *she made our house a home.*
> *But what can you say of Mother?*
>> *There's so much there to say!*
> *How can you tell of a lifetime*
>> *in any other way?*
> *You can talk of grace and beauty;*
>> *you can talk of love and care,*
> *But unless you knew my mother,*
>> *you wouldn't see them there.*
> *For her grace was in her constant work*
>> *to serve her family.*
> *Her beauty was her inner strength*
>> *we relied on heavily.*
> *A life of service, we are told,*
>> *will keep you young forever.*
> *This was surely true of Mom;*
>> *she never stopped serving ever.*
> *And she could take the biggest hurts*
>> *and bring them down to size,*
> *With a smile and a kiss and a prayer,*
>> *and a look from her loving eyes.*
> *For no job was too big for Mother,*
>> *or too long or boring or hard.*
> *She would patiently keep on working,*
>> *and leave the results to God.*
> *And that's how she worked with her children,*
>> *Loving each in her own special way,*
> *Giving to them from her storehouse*
>> *The best that she had every day.*

## MAY 14

Mom and Dad have come up with a creative solution for what to do with Linda the year that Linda is in kindergarten. She spends her mornings with Dad at the store. She loves "helping" him go through all of his routines to open the store, the dusting of everything, the sweeping the floor with the wide broom and the stinky red powder, the winding down of the awnings. She spends many hours writing and drawing at her little silver desk, adds columns of numbers on the adding machine, and pretends she is talking with Betty Grable on the telephone.

Sometimes she goes back to the repair shop to visit with Uncle Johnny, and she can spend a great deal of time back in the corner listening to children's records of stories and songs. If she's not there, she can be found clutching Dad's leg and peaking out from behind. She's so quiet; they never hear a peep out of her. Aunt Millie takes her to the lunch counter at Kresges' for an egg salad sandwich, and then she is off to afternoon kindergarten. Linda seems to enjoy the time at the store and is causing no trouble, Mom really likes being back to teaching, and we can use the extra income, so it has worked out very well.

## MAY 15

The sandman is supposed to come and put you to sleep at night, which accounts for why you have sand in the corner of your eyes in the morning. Our sandman has a tough row to hoe. We were really giddy last night. Dad was furious with us after awhile, so he put his foot down, letting us know we had gone past the limit. That was when we stopped giggling, and let the sandman have his way.

## MAY 16

Sometimes our little house is so hectic and noisy and crowded with stuff everywhere that it nearly drives us crazy. Each of us needs to find a getaway, a place to be alone... to think, to dream, to plan, to pray, to be our own person.

Here's how we each do it:

-You can tell by the faraway look in her eyes, that Mom goes somewhere else while she irons. The repetitive movements are conducive to that.

-Dad gets up in the middle of the night, spending hours and hours at the breakfast nook alone, reading, thinking, figuring.

-Marcia needs to be outside, where there is light and air. She escapes to the front porch, often with a coloring book and crayons.

-Marilyn is a reader, so she grabs a book and a chair and is gone.

-Sharon goes down to the basement and works things out by tap dancing; eventually that pent up energy she has in her dissipates. She also goes out to the Hamilton's swing and licks her wounds at times.

-Linda imagines her own room in the attic, a room, with chintz curtains and bedspread. It's beautiful and quiet and orderly.

## MAY 17

It's Friday. We stopped by McGrath's Fish Market on the way home from the store. We always eat fish on Fridays because we can't eat meat. * We leave the bright light and warmth of the spring day to enter the little white cement-block building with blue trim. The big door is heavy and metal, insulated. It chomps shut behind us like a trap, bringing a little shiver. The air is cold, and the smell of fish is strong, like the smell of the lake in Wisconsin. White and blue neon lights cast an eerie glow on the large oval metal tanks full of ice chips with various fish lying on top. Some are whole with their silvery iridescent skins, and bulging eyes staring up at you, one after another. Others are naked slabs, skin and bones removed, all pink or white, and shiny, layer upon layer. There is a mound of gray shrimp.

We see the waxy round containers used for bringing fresh oysters home, when Dad gets hungry for oyster stew, but this is not a day for us to have to endure oyster stew. Today is a *good* day, for it's spring, and the fresh-water smelt have been running. Tonight Mom will fry us up some crunchy little smelt, one of our favorites. Mom lets us each get a big fat dill pickle out of the clear barrel-shaped jar, so Mr. McGrath wraps them in little wax wrappers and hands them to us. He is a stocky man in a white paper sailor's hat and white apron. His hands are large and red from handling cold fish all day.

Sharry has been waiting outside. She loves to go back and forth balancing on the low pipe that serves as a barrier to keep cars off the grass.

*[Catholics during this era were forbidden to eat meat on Fridays. Even the schools served fish in their lunch programs on Fridays.]

**MAY 18**

While we were out working in the backyard garden today, Dorothy Friederich, our neighbor across the street, stopped by on her way to church. She said she couldn't stay, for she only had a minute. At that, Mom squeezed my hand to say we knew better. We know what a talker she is. She left two hours later. Mom stopped what she was doing to listen. With Dorothy, you really can't get a word in edgewise. After she left, Mom said she had wanted to finish what we were doing, but friends are very important, and sometimes their needs have to come first. Dorothy is a dear friend of ours, and that work will always wait, getting done in its own time. We finished the weeding after she left.

[Mom had a massive coronary, dying while she was on an AARP bus trip with Dorothy. We were grateful for Dorothy's talkativeness, for she told us every detail, which is very comforting under such circumstances. At our mother's wake, I lost count of the number of people who said to me, "Your mother was the best friend I ever had." A constant stream of people came by to pay their last respects from four in the afternoon until nine-thirty in the evening. No wonder. Friendship was a very high priority for her. She was a busy woman with many responsibilities, but she would always make time for a friend.]

**MAY 19**

Dad said he thought he wouldn't go to mass today because it was raining. We didn't think that counted for a legitimate reason to stay home. We hoped he wouldn't die and go to hell on account of it. He said he'd have church on the radio.

In the afternoon, the weather cleared up, so the twins walked over to Aunt Millie's, to spend the afternoon with her. Sharry went off to play baseball at the park. She can hit the ball better than most of the boys; she tries so hard to be the boy Dad never had!

Linda was feeling pretty forlorn, but Mom said there was no need to feel down in the dumps about that. "Let's make the best of it," she said. "Who knows? We may even have more fun than they are having. We are going to do something very special, just the two of us. How would that be? How would you like to learn something none of the other girls even know how to do? Would you like to learn how to crochet? Why, when we were girls we made scarves and hats, and all sorts of things by crocheting." Boy, that sounded like just the ticket to Linda. So the afternoon flew by as Mom patiently taught her how to wield a crochet hook in and out of the holes created with the yarn.

[Linda has enjoyed crocheting and knitting all of her life, and it started on this special day. None of the other girls ever learned how to do it, nor cared to learn for that matter, I suppose.]

*Whatever happens, let's just make the best of it.*

**MAY 20**

[Historical note:  An amazing insight from Sharon, 2008]

Linda observed every small detail there was to be noticed, but I took that all away from her with one careless act in the sandbox. I shoveled too hard, and flipped the sand right into her eye. Since a cat had used the sandbox for a litter box, her eye got infected, and now she's almost blind in that eye. It's all my fault! I shouldn't be so careless like that. How could I? I never intended to hurt her; I really didn't. We were just playing and having fun, and then it just happened. But now, it's all my fault! I'm her big sister; I'm stronger, so I can dig harder and faster. I'm supposed to protect her from harm, not cause it!

The castle we were intending to build never was built, for she had to be rushed to the emergency room, have several operations on her eye, and to this day can see very little out of that eye. Her poor eye-hand coordination got even worse for all times. Poor Linda, blind in one eye. Fortunately, she still loves me. Poor sister Sharry, living with the guilt all these years... or forever.

The rest of the story:

When I was sixty-five, fifty-seven years after this accident happened, Linda and I were discussing this incident. I was telling her how sorry I was that I had caused her to be blind in that eye. "What?" she said. "What ever gave you that idea?"

Here is her story of what really happened:

It was the year I spent with Dad when I was in kindergarten. He had gone to deliver an appliance to

a home with children, and had me with him. I was
invited to play with the children in their sandbox
while he installed the appliance. During the play, a
little piece of sand got in my eye. Of course, not knowing any better, I rubbed it, and caused a scratch on
the cornea. Because a cat had used the sandbox, and I
had the scratch, that set me up for an infection. I had
to go to the hospital (not rushed by ambulance to the
emergency room) where I had antibiotics for a time
(a few days or maybe a week). I had to wear a patch
and continue the antibiotics at home. Because there
is a scar on the cornea, I have impaired vision that is
corrected somewhat by glasses. Sharry was not at the
accident scene and was not responsible in any way for
what happened. It's true that I have poor eye hand
coordination.   Oh, well.

*There's no use crying over spilled milk.*

**MAY 21**

High school band and choral concert day has finally
arrived. Everyone is excited. Seems like Marcia has
been sucking on those saxophone reeds for weeks, and
Marilyn has been going over and over her words and
tunes.  We have Marilyn's white blouse and black skirt
ironed, and Marcia has bought extra reeds, just in
case. Our small bathroom is a busy place when we are
all getting ready for something at once. We help each
other with hair; hairdos have to be just right, and the
twins are old enough to fuss with make-up now, too.
Mom comes to see her big girls in the concert with the
little girls at her side. Dad may come too, or maybe
not. All goes well. We all go home quite satisfied, and
both glad and sad that it's over.

**MAY 22**

The twins have been working for the last six weeks on their bug collections for Biology class. We are all helping to collect the bugs, turning over rocks to find beetles, and catching butterflies with nets the twins have made by bending a coat hanger into a circle, sewing an old lace curtain onto it like a sack, and then attaching it to an old broom handle. Pretty cool. After we catch the bugs, they go into a jar with a cotton ball that has fingernail polish remover on it. That puts them to sleep. Well, actually, they go to sleep and then they die. Next, they are skewered with long T-pins, right through the thorax. On a beetle, that's not easy to do, their shells are so hard! Sometimes in the process, their legs fall off and have to be glued back on, so they look right. That's kind of creepy, and gives us the giggles, but you should see the butterflies. They are so beautiful!

Once they are pinned, the bugs are made into a display in a cigar box, with all of their information written out neatly below. In biology, all living things are classified according to their characteristics, and are given a Latin name. Each is part of a kingdom, a phylum, a class, an order, a family, a genus, and a species. The butterflies are part of the Lepidoptera order. The word "Lepidoptera" has a neat sound, doesn't it? Spiders are arachnids. People are *homo sapiens*.

*Let me put a bee in your bonnet.*

(This actually has nothing to do with bugs. It means, let me give you an idea.)

**MAY 23**

At long last, the bug collections were turned in today. Mom was very relieved. Our house is just too small to have zillions of jars full of dead bugs all over the place. She is not too crazy about insects anyway.

**MAY 24**

In school, the teachers are working us really hard. They are trying to get their final licks in. We are not responding too well because we all have spring fever. Mom said that all of her students had "ants in their pants" today. Of course that means they just couldn't sit still and concentrate. We are definitely sick of school, and ready to be full time loafers.

This week we have been doing Stanford-Binet Achievement tests. You have to have two yellow #2 lead pencils, sharpened and ready to go, as the tests are timed. They make you a little nervous, but we kind of like to take them. We know we will do pretty well. We're smart.

[When Sharry played marbles with the boys in the empty lot next to Greeley School, she really did get ants in her pants, and it would drive her crazy. They bit sometimes, too.]

**MAY 25**

As we are drawing to the end of the school year, we begin thinking all the more about our job working at Gotch Radio Specialties, since we move to working a great deal more hours in the summer. There is no way to overestimate the value that we, as a family, gain from having a family business. First of all, as a family, it gives us a common goal, something we are all pulling together on to make it happen. The fact that we are doing this with each other as well as with an aunt and uncle makes it just that much richer. As a family, we have an identity; we know what we are about. We are about providing the people of our town with an enjoyable way to bring the beauty and fun of music into their lives.

## MAY 26

We girls love to work at the store. It is fun and interesting and challenging at times. Even on slow days, it isn't so bad because that is the time we use to familiarize ourselves with the inventory so if anyone asks if we have a certain record, we usually know before we look if we have it or not. We know exactly where to find it, and if we are out of it, we know something similar that the customer might like to buy instead.

While we are studying the inventory, we note if we are low on something or out of it, and let Dad know that he should order it. We know that is a big help to him. We know he is depending on us to give him good information. All of that makes us feel very good about ourselves. Dad trusts us and knows we will be responsible.

## MAY 27

We never really think about it this way, but we are doing on-the-job training for how to be successful in business. At a very early age, we know what it takes to earn money to be able to buy the things you want or need. It's called "hard work."

*Work is good for you; hard work never hurt anyone.*

[Historical note: The fact that our business wasn't a success in the end, and that we never got anything out of the sale of it is totally irrelevant to us. We learned some life lessons that were priceless. Those lessons might have been more important than our college educations.]

## MAY 28

What a great privilege we have, for we are involved in our mother's world by the fact that we are in school all during the school year, and we are involved in our father's world all summer. We are very aware of the challenges they face on a day-to-day basis, and can really celebrate with understanding the victories. We know that our willingness to support them by being good kids is a big factor in their ability to do what they need to do. We benefit from their work, and they benefit from ours. They are counting on us as much as we are counting on them.

## MAY 29

At the shop, we are learning that to be successful, you can't just have a good product, you have to give good service, and to give good service, you have to think of others. So we are learning to think of others. How can we help our customers find just what they are looking for, or just the right gift?

If it turns out that a record is defective, which happens now and then, we are certainly glad to replace it. If we fix a radio, but it still doesn't work right, the customer should bring it back, and Uncle Johnny will fix it for no further charge. There is great value, no doubt, in learning to consider the needs and wants of others.

## MAY 30

Some kind of music appeals to every kind of person. Children come in for music to laugh and learn from, teens come for music to help them navigate the ups and downs of growing up, sweethearts need music to express the depth of their love, and then sometimes, if it doesn't work out, to help them wring out their broken hearts. The hillbillies need something to ride their motorcycles to and some melodic tragic stories to put their problems in perspective. There are some folks who want someone to help them sing the blues. Some come in to find music to help them worship God, and others want to be patriotic.

Some of our customers love to dance, or to remember the days when they went to the dance pavilions, so they buy the Big Band sounds. Some people want to remember the wonderful time they had going to the theatre or a movie, so we carry show tunes and sound tracks. If you want to have some fun and dance a polka, we have the biggest and best polka selection in the area. Some sophisticated people want to soar to higher ground, so they buy some lofty classical album. A few people want to be really cool, so they buy jazz.

If you want to laugh, we have some recordings by Flip Wilson and Spike Jones, and, God forbid, if you want some dirty humor, Dad could show you something by Redd Fox. If you are out of shape, you might want to get a Paul Fogarty exercise album. And if you are old, and you have lost your mate, you might come in and get the songs that you have shared together and cry until you are all cried out. Whatever you want or need musically, whatever kind of person you are, young or old, rich or poor, we are here to serve you. And we love helping. May we help you?

*To each his own;*
*it takes all kinds of people to make up a world.*

**MAY 31**

Mom wasn't cheerfully singing "Oh What a Beautiful Morning" today, as she often does. She has been working on report cards in the evenings, and worrying about the students in her class. It is obvious that she's going to have to fail one or two. "If they can't do the work, they really shouldn't go on." That's what she says. She works very hard to help everyone succeed, but some children don't get enough support from home, and some of them are lazy and won't work hard. Part of school is just plain hard work, and not fun at all. Today marked the end of the last full week of school. It won't be long now!

*You can lead a horse to water,*
*but you can't make him drink.*

# Hooray!

# It's May!

Linda at her desk.

BBQ in the park

Linda spends
kindergarden
mornings with
her daddy at
the Gotch Radio

*Maypole Dance at Oakland Park School*

*Dorothy and Hulda, friends for life*

*Chills and Thrills*

**JUNE 1**

The last Saturday before school is out. (Yea!)   The
last Saturday that we have Catechism (Yea!)  The last
Saturday before Sharry's ballet (Oh, boy!)  No drum
lesson today, since the band concert is over. (That's a
break!)

Mom is working all day today on grades, report
cards, attendance records, etc. On each report card,
she writes a personal note letting the parents know
her thoughts on how the child has progressed through
the year, their strengths to be praised and their
weaknesses to be worked on over the summer. It is
very time-consuming and takes a great deal of concentration. We either have to work quietly on something
or play outdoors.  It is a nice warm day, so we play
outdoors.

*It was so quiet, you could hear a pin drop.*

**JUNE 2**

One year, 1952, the twins graduate from eighth grade at Plumb School on this day. They are dressed alike for the occasion, and are so proud of their new gold Elgin watches that are all the go. Soon they will go to high school. They are getting so grown up! Everyone is proud of them. Some of our aunts and uncles never finished high school. They had to quit in order to go to work and support the family.

**MONDAY, JUNE 3, THE LAST WEEK OF SCHOOL**

It was the very last day to return overdue school library books today. The borrower has to pay for any not returned. Last night, Marcia was in deep trouble. She had three books missing. Mom set up an incentive to encourage us all to help find the missing books. The reward: five gold stars.

We all fell for it. Sharon found one that had fallen behind the bed. Marilyn discovered that she had one of them mixed up with her school stuff. After a long time, Linda found the third one, proving Mom's saying that the best way to find something is to clean the house. Linda went to move a stack of Dad's newspapers off of the breakfast nook, and under the pile was the missing book. Happy ending. Marcia turned in all three books today, with no fines, and we have more gold stars!

*The best way to find something*
*is to clean the house.*
*Every good deed deserves a gold star.*

**TUESDAY, JUNE 4**
It was the next to the last day of school. We spent a good deal of the day checking our textbooks in after we erased all of the pencil marks, which had gotten on many of the pages. It makes you glad that you were generally careful, and it makes you realize as you look through the pages, how very much we learned this year. We hardly knew anything when we started and now we know all that!!

**WEDNESDAY, JUNE 5           LAST DAY OF SCHOOL**
Yippee! *"School's out, School's out. Teacher let the monkeys out! One went in, one went out, one went in the teacher's mouth."* That's our silly song we sing as we skip home.

They handed out the end of the year report cards today, of course.   Sharon got straight A's, as usual. Dad expects her to get straight A's. That's the deal they made. The rest of us get mostly B's with a few A's and C's mixed in. We're all pretty good students. Mom doesn't necessarily want us to be straight A students. She wants us to be well rounded, and not just have our noses to the grindstone all the time.

Exception: Marilyn received a D in PE.
Dad just can't understand how anyone can get a D in P.E. " Is it so hard just to go out and play ball?" he wondered out loud.  For Marilyn it is hard to do such things. She's a little overweight, and not very coordinated. When the ball comes, it scares her, so she backs away, closes her eyes, and swings with all her might, all the way around. She can't catch either, so there is no use putting her in the outfield. That will get you a D every time.

Marilyn just shrugged her shoulders. It didn't really bother her that much.

[To be fair in our reporting, Linda once received a D in PE as well. It must have been some sport, like baseball, that takes the vision of two eyes to do it well.]

*You can't get blood out of a turnip.*

## THURSDAY, JUNE 6
*"No more teachers. No more books. No more teachers' dirty looks."* That's our silly rhyme.

It is the first day of summer vacation. What are we going to do with it? We want to just play, play, play, play, play. And read books from the library. And go on fun vacations to Bloomington and Wisconsin. And never think about school for a long, long time…three whole months! Mom says it will go by fast enough, but right now it feels like forever. One thing we love about summer is that we have our mother all to ourselves, no sharing with the other children at school, except sometimes when a child comes over to be tutored, but that is not very often.

We spent the first half hour today finding the skate key. Then we roller-skated all morning. We're kind of rusty on doubles. Holding hands, Sharon goes backward, skates weaving out and in and in and out while Linda pushes from the forward position. The one going forward, of course, has to be sure you're not skating right into or over something. We were skating on the sidewalk with our metal skates, but later in the summer, we might go out to the skating rink. It's fun to play "crack the whip" on the skates that lace up. If you have a long line of kids, you swing a far ways out!

**FRIDAY, JUNE 7**
We played outdoors all day again today, so we were
tired and dirty at the end of the day. "Good night.
Sleep tight. Don't let the bedbugs bite," we said, with a
giggle. Is there really such a thing as a bedbug? We've
never seen one.

**SATURDAY, JUNE 8**
Vacation. Mom let us sleep in. Finally she woke us
up with, "Up and at 'em." She needed us to all pitch in
and clean the house this morning. So we did. Marcia
cut the grass. Marilyn did laundry. Sharry ran the
vacuum and dusted. Linda scrubbed the kitchen and
bathroom floors.
We didn't want to work, but like Mom says, "We
have the whole delicious summer ahead of us to be
lazy." She is busy finishing up Sharry's ballet costumes. Final hard practice is this afternoon, dress
rehearsal is next Sunday, and then the ballet is on
Monday and Tuesday evenings. Sharry is excited,
going over and over her routines. No catechism today,
thank God! No other lessons of any kind.

**SUNDAY, JUNE 9**
Church. Sunday Dinner Roast with potatoes and
carrots. Lazy afternoon naps, then the first summer
trip to the library this afternoon on our bikes. We
love the library! Tonight we played Kick the Can after
supper in the alley behind Allen's. The days are long
now, so it was a nice long game. All of the neighbor
kids joined in. There must have been ten or twelve of
us. Then we headed for home. We all know we have

to be home by dark. Finally, it's really summer! Even
the lightening bugs came out, which was perfect.

**MONDAY, JUNE 10**

There's no putting it off; deep spring-cleaning
always gets done in the summer. Every closet, shelf
and drawer, every blanket, rug, wall and window,
every Venetian blind will get cleaned and organized
through the course of the summer. Last of all will
be the jam-packed China cabinet. This year we're
starting in the kitchen, beginning at the top and
working down. Sharon rarely volunteers for indoor
manual labor, but this time she did. She likes to do
the spice cupboard above the stove. She'll get her turn
out of the way.

The rest of us can fight over who does what, and
Mom will do some jobs peacefully all by herself. She
loves this rather mindless work, where you can see
measurable results the same day, so different from her
teaching. The rest of us were free to go and play outdoors. Linda rode her bike up and down the street a
million times and ended up running through the hose
to cool down. The twins were off somewhere.

*Cleanliness is next to godliness.*

**TUESDAY, JUNE 11**

All the kitchen cupboards holding glassware and
plates were cleaned today. The twins did that with
Mom, because all that stuff can break. And you can
see the counter top again. Progress. Sharon and Linda
packed up all the empty pop bottles from the basement
into the wagon, and took them back to the grocery
store for a refund. "60/40 split on the money," Sharry

said, "because it was her idea." Linda wasn't sure what 60/40 meant, but she was happy with the little bit Sharry gave her to buy some penny candy at the little neighborhood grocery. We got a loaf of bread for Mom while we were there, twenty cents.

We dug out all of the dead light bulbs from the year, too, and one of these days we will take them to the electric company to exchange them for new ones. It's another one of our jobs.

**WEDNESDAY, JUNE 12**
Mom cleaned the oven today with SOS, and the burner pans. The oven racks look so nice and shiny. It took all morning, but it was worth it. It won't have to be done again for a long time.

When we cleaned out the bottles yesterday, we found some old chalk in the basement, so we decided to play hopscotch. * First, we hunted up some broken glass from the alley to use for markers. The best markers are pieces from the bottoms of Coke bottles. They are really heavy and sit down when you throw them to the right spot. If they are from the alley, they don't have sharp edges anymore; they're all smoothed out. We played hopscotch for a long time. Some of the neighbor kids came over so we had a pretty good game going with lots of competition. That's what Sharry likes. Linda can hold her own at hopscotch. By afternoon, though, we switched to jacks* for a while. No competition there. Sharon wins hands down.

Mom is still sewing sequins on Sharry's costumes this evening, but she's almost finished. All of the neighborhood kids were up for Hide and Seek, so that's what we did all evening.

*See Appendix D

## THURSDAY, JUNE 13

The spring -cleaning of the house continues. Today was bottom cupboards, scrubbing all of the pans with SOS until they were shiny again, pitching all of the miscellaneous bits of this and that that had accumulated under the sink with the paper grocery sacks and cleaning supplies, and wiping under the bottles of sticky stuff like the dark corn syrup, the grape jelly jar, and the Crème de Menthe in the liquor section to the right of the sink. Linda was the helper.

## FRIDAY, JUNE 14

The Gotch girls are all fond of visiting with neighbors, sometimes to Mom's chagrin. She doesn't want us to be a pest for our neighbors, but Sharon spends countless hours next door with Matty. They have developed a relationship of mutual respect and admiration. When her spirits get all bent out of shape at home, off she goes to her sounding board, her understanding, gentle, but firm "father." When her "I know everything" attitude gets too much for him, he knows just how to bring her back to reality. " Just remember," he says, " going to school doesn't make you smart."

[Linda had a similar relationship with our neighbor, Pete, starting in high school. Since we had a Dad that was largely absent due to his work schedule, tavern schedule, and sleep patterns, it is only natural that we would seek out mentor / father substitutes. The twins had no need of this kind of relationship because Dad was around more and was more involved when they were young.]

Linda and the twins all like to visit the old ladies in the neighborhood, too, now and again. Old people get lonely and like to have little visitors occasionally.

The last sequin and last stitch went into the ballet costumes tonight. Mom met her deadline with a day to spare.

*Perseverance pays.*

SATURDAY, JUNE 15

Summer means more time to spend with neighbors as a family, too. It was a nice sunny day for the annual neighborhood cookout in our backyard, with Matt, Lou, and Jane from next door, and Pete from down the street. Because he has lived next door to the Big House forever, Pete's sons played baseball with Dad when they were all growing up. Pete lost his wife Grace while she was still quite young, so he lives alone, and we love to have him come spend some time with us. He is quite funny and entertaining.

Somewhere in the backyard, our yard turns into the Hamilton's side yard. We don't exactly know where because it doesn't really matter. Lucille brought homegrown sliced tomatoes from her father's garden. They were so good! Her father is blind, but he still has a huge garden, and does all of his own baking. That is so amazing to us! Mom made her famous baked beans. Everything was good.

SUNDAY, JUNE 16

Church. No Sunday Dinner. Sharry 's ballet dress

rehearsal is all afternoon. Mom has to be there, also. She lines up the ballerinas and dancers, getting them ready to go on stage, keeping them quiet until it's their turn. It went pretty well. Miss Hupp was extra stern. All it took was one child messing up and getting an angry warning that if she did it again she would not get to perform in the show to have everyone else be on their best behavior and level of concentration.

The twins stayed with Linda today while Mom and Sharon were at the rehearsal. Mom had bought a new book of paper dolls for her, so Marcia helped her cut them all out, making sure the tabs didn't get cut off accidentally, which Linda has a tendency to do. Marilyn hates paper dolls. She cleaned the kitchen from lunch, and read a novel all afternoon.    After the paper dolls, Marcia and Linda colored in coloring books until the others returned.

Sharon was edgy and snippy, one minute bragging about what a good job she had done, but the next fearful that she wouldn't be absolutely perfect for the actual performances.  We had to give her a wide berth.

MONDAY, JUNE 17
Opening night of the ballet was tonight. Very exciting. The music, the lights, the action. Sharry was radiant with the excitement of it all. Around the breakfast nook , when they were back home,  she recounted every detail to all of us who are coming tomorrow night, especially her aggravation for the few slip-ups that occurred due to other's lack of perfection.

TUESDAY, JUNE 18
The last night of the ballet. Mom was backstage, but the rest of us were all out in the audience, even

Dad. It was such a great show. They do amazing things with their bodies! Linda thinks it must be wonderful to be so talented and coordinated! We are so proud of Sharry! She always seems to be the best one in her group. Maybe we're prejudiced about that. The costumes were so sparkly and colorful! Mom said seeing her up there made all of the hours of sewing worthwhile.

There is a financial sacrifice as well, for dance lessons are quite expensive. Aunt Martha originally offered to pay for them, but she must have forgotten the offer, for she's never paid a penny. Somehow Mom finds the money. Sometimes we have to do without material things so that we can have experiences and education. It's a good trade.

[We were still walking on the threadbare carpet in the living room, and had the same well-worn furniture when the last of us finished college.]

### WEDNESDAY, JUNE 19

Sharry must have been dancing and doing acrobatics in her dreams last night. Marcia said she was all over the bed, kicking even worse than usual. Their sheets were a mess in the morning. It didn't help that it was such a warm night. We had the window wide open, but there is no cross draft to bring us relief. The June bugs were making noise banging into the screen, too, so it was a long night on their side of the room. Marilyn and Linda never heard a thing, but slept soundly as ever.

### THURSDAY, JUNE 20

Mom's glad to have the ballet behind her, but

Sharry will be riding high for a few days at least. She gave a stellar performance, and she knows it. Now she'll probably dream of being a professional dancer someday. Dad doesn't really like ballet. He thinks the boy dancers are all sissies. He didn't say anything after the ballet, though, but just went right to bed when we got home.

**FRIDAY, JUNE 21**

The circus is coming to town! The circus is coming to town! They came by to put posters in the store window today. Dad asked Sharry if she wanted to go with him again to see the set-up early in the morning. She jumped at the chance. They love the circus. It is their special time to share. Sharry is definitely Dad's little circus pal. Years ago, the twins went with him; they were his circus pals, too.

[Linda only went once. That was enough for her.]

*Never a dull moment.*

**SATURDAY, JUNE 22**

That was just the spark of inspiration we needed to get Sharry planning our yearly roller skating extravaganza with a circus theme. Of course, Sharry will be the star of the show. Since she's a dancer, she can skate well, also. We have other skaters in our neighborhood that can do some amazing tricks, too. Even Linda can do a few simple tricks.

Linda was busy with her Saturday Fun Club this morning. Jane, Beverly, Karen and Dee Dee were over to watch "Mighty Mouse" and "My Friend Flicka" with her and then they had hamburgers. It's a fun little time they have, with lots of giggles.

**SUNDAY, JUNE 23   FATHER'S DAY**
Today we honored our dad by giving him a new tie. He wears a suit and tie to work every day with his perfectly-ironed starched shirt; he looks so snazzy as he goes off to his business "on Main Street" as Mom says, though our store isn't exactly on Main Street.

[Happy Father's Day, Dad. You made our lives more difficult at times, but we still love you. We're sorry that we actually didn't get to know the *real* you, the man Mom was so proud of and loved so dearly. You seemed a different father to each of us. Marcia says this, " I know I was your favorite, and I cherish those special memories." We think Marilyn would have this to say, "You were always very proud of me. Thanks for helping me feel so confident." Sharry says, "I know that no matter how much I loved you, I never felt I was able to please you. Perhaps Mom said it best when she said, 'You two are just too much alike to get along, both too stubborn,' and I am still that way. If you were alive today, I would still stand up to you and feel proud, but hopefully in wiser ways." And Linda's response? "What dad? The one I *wished* I had? Being the last, I kind of missed out, didn't I?"
Dad was a man whose heart was good and integrity strong, but whose ways were hard to understand, and sometimes wrong.]

**MONDAY, JUNE 24**
"The Greatest Show on Earth" The One and Only

Circus Show on Skates  Right in your own neighborhood  (McIntosh's Driveway) Death defying feats of
danger!  See it with your own eyes!  Only 1 cent.
This Wednesday  June 26  4 p.m.  So read the hand-
bills we wrote up by hand and passed out around the
neighborhood.

## TUESDAY, JUNE 25

We are working feverishly to prepare for our skating
show, figuring out costumes and how to do the music,
who will do which tricks and when. Sharry is in
charge, directing everyone else. A record player can
play some circus music we got from the store. That
should do it. It's all coming together.

## WEDNESDAY, JUNE 26

Six little kids put on the skating show of a lifetime
today. Jack made a great little ringmaster in his
father's old red blazer, and his grandfather's top hat.
"Ladies and Gentlemen...." he announced. Sharry
looked like a trapeze artist in her resplendent dancing
costume, flying and twirling on skates, amazing the
audience, arms wide to the side, and one leg extended
out behind. Jane and Marsha skated double, making
lots of turns, teeter tottering up and down. Linda was
incognito as the clown in the Halloween outfit, with
lipstick on her nose.

After a little juggling of colorful bean bags by the
ringmaster, the Allen's dog, Bingo, in one of Sharon's
tutus, brought the house down as he walked on two
legs with just a little help. The finale was truly grand.
All six of us, on our skates, joined hands and wound
our way in snakelike fashion down the steepest part
of the driveway, coming dangerously close to the

ongoing traffic just beyond the edge of the driveway. The music played on and on. The applause from the audience – a few friends and neighbors – made it all worthwhile, and we'll use the pennies to buy a bit of candy over at Goluba's store.

**THURSDAY, JUNE 27**

After all the excitement of our skating show over, and the real circus just ahead, it was almost a welcome change to quietly sit and dig the weeds out of the brick sidewalk out front today. We did it together, each doing a section, our hands busy with the screwdrivers, our minds occupied with thoughts and dreams. What would it be like to run away from home and join the circus???

A third of our vacation, one month, is almost over. We can't believe it, but there is plenty more to come. We're reading our way through whole shelves of the children's book section at the library. We're weaving plastic lacing into bracelets down in the Hub at the YMCA. The twins are really good at it. Mom is teaching Linda to sew doll clothes by hand. It's the same thing Mom did when she was a girl, so Linda loves that. She is also learning to embroider pillowcases. Marcia helps her learn all of the special stitches, how to split up the thread, and how to attach the hoop to the material. They enjoy doing this sort of thing together. Mom has also taught Linda to do the whip stitch, which is the one you use for mending and hemming. She's already pretty good at it.

*A stitch in time saves nine.*

[We have the doll clothes Mom made circa 1916 and

a few things made by Linda. They sewed together occasionally until Mom died in 1979. Linda has hemmed and mended and made her own clothes and household items all of her life with great satisfaction.]

### FRIDAY, JUNE 28
In the eerie pre-dawn fog, Daddy and I (Sharry) steel silently through the tall damp grass moving ever closer to the clank of the sledgehammers, staking out the lot. Drawn to and repelled by the fetid steamy presence of the arrogant camels, we move on past spindly-legged giraffes and swaying llamas grazing peacefully on their tethers.

In the distance, we see the silhouettes of the elephants, large and lumbering on their tree-trunk feet. By all this bigness, I am small, and yet by being there, I am a part of the bigness. A loud roar startles me into realizing that we have made our way into a maze of wagons holding the big cats, the lions and tigers. Pacing and growling, roaring louder than thunder, they make me shiver, and Daddy's warm hand squeezes mine more tightly. I'm safe with him.

We move toward the uproar of yelling bosses and stomping horses, the scrape of heavy canvas sliding over itself. I can hardly breathe with the excitement of it all. Like a sleeping giant arising from a great nap, the big top goes up, and the best is yet to come.

### SATURDAY, JUNE 29    CIRCUS DAY
Uncle Jeff, who is a clown, has been reminiscing with us about the old days when the circus paraded down Main Street, jugglers and trapeze artists in their tights and fish net hose, high stepping horses dancing to the calliope, elephants tied together by

their tails, big fat clowns with red ball noses, little tiny clowns with big feet, and tall clowns on stilts all being silly together, after colorful wagons of lions and tigers, and after all of the animals in the menagerie. Hearing all of this, we are eager to experience the circus for ourselves.

"Step right up. Get your tickets here," we hear as we are herded into the Big Top. "Popcorn" "Roasted peanuts" "Cotton candy" "Get it here" Front row seats. "Ladies and Gentlemen" the Ringmaster announces, and the show begins. Who can see it all? Spotlights flash here and there, round and round. Wonderful things are happening everywhere. Crunching on peanuts, and letting the shells fall where they may, we are spellbound, stilled with fascination. First there's one thrill, and then another, and another and another, each more spectacular than the last! How do they do these impossible things? We hope it will never end. Emmett Kelly, we think, sweeps the spotlight into a tiny little pile, and we all go home with sticky hands and big, big smiles.

**SUNDAY, JUNE 30**

The breakfast nook was humming with stories today all about what we saw and felt, heard and smelled at the circus, each one talking as fast as she could, interrupting and outdoing the other for the magnitude of all we had experienced. "Did you see this?" Did you see that?" we asked each other, for it is impossible to see what is going on in all three rings at once. The noise level rose with each description. "Don't talk so loud," Mom said, trying to hush us. "They'll hear you all the way to Main Street." Such a big month, and next month promises to be even better!

# Summer Thoughts and Memories

It's Summer!

Rosalind Hupp's

# BALLET

MONDAY AND TUESDAY
JUNE 18 AND 19, 1951
8:00 P.M.

HIGH SCHOOL AUDITORIUM
STREATOR, ILLINOIS

*Happy Travels*

**THURSDAY, JULY 1**

    With the circus over, summer at home is all of a sudden very boring. It's a warm afternoon; Mom is ironing anyway. She creases the pants just right, and each ruffle is turned along the front edge of the iron. She is watching the Cubbies while she works. Sharon is flopped on the couch watching the game, too. The twins are across the street visiting their friend Leila Ashlock. They don't care about the Cubs, for they are White Sox fans like Dad. Linda has little interest in baseball at all. She can't remember if 2 and 0 means 2 balls and no strikes or 2 strikes and no balls. The only player she can remember is Mickey Mantle, who is a NY Yankee. The Cubs are losing again, of course.

**FRIDAY, JULY 2**

    Today Mom is packing things for our trip to Bloomington. Several times per year, we drive down

Rt. 66 to see Mom's side of the family. Sharon and
Linda will be staying two weeks with Aunt Martha
and Uncle Clarence, so Sharon is extremely excited.
She loves to visit them, for they spoil her unbelievably,
and adore everything she does and says. When Sharon
was little, Mom hurt her leg, and was unable to walk,
so she could not take care of her for a time. Aunt
Martha and Uncle Clarence graciously took the little
one to Bloomington to care for her. That special time
started a love between them that is deep and lasting.

Linda loves to go to Bloomington, too, but the
prospect of a whole week away from her Mom always
frightens her. After all, she is a whole two and a half
years younger. She is quiet all morning, clinging to
Mom. "She'll be fine once she gets there," Mom says.

SATURDAY, JULY 3

Dad has to work today, so we'll drive down to
Bloomington tomorrow. That is good for us because we
can go to the Fourth of July carnival before we leave.
It is always exciting when the carnival comes to town.
We look forward to riding on the Ferris wheel, so high
above the crowds. It takes your breath away when it
goes over the top and starts down! We love the Tilt-
a-whirl, too, that makes us dizzy, and the Scrambler,
that forces us to smash into each other at every turn.
[This was especially fun to do with a boyfriend, as we
got older.]

You can't beat the smells of the hot sugar being
spun into cotton candy, and the sweet icy goodness of
a snow cone, but Dad loves the foot long hot dogs with
lots of mustard. We throw pennies across the aisle to
land in dishes and flip little wooden rings onto the
top of cola bottles in order to win soft cotton Indian

blankets, though we hardly ever win. The toy ducks we pick out of the water always get us a Chinese woven finger trap or some other junky thing, too, instead of a stuffed animal, but we don't care. It's fun anyway. Still, we always hope someone will win us a bear. Carnival people are a little creepy to us with all of their icky tattoos and missing teeth, but that only adds to the strange and wonderful nature of it all.

[No one ever did win us a bear. Oh, well.]

## SUNDAY, JULY 4

After Mass, we headed out for Bloomington. Sharry had trouble sitting still on the trip down. She had a hundred ideas racing through her head about all we might do this week, with Fourth of July celebrations being part of it. She and the twins are in the back. Linda is safely snuggled up to Mom on the front seat of the car. It is a long, long, long one-hour drive. At last we pull up to their large, elegant home. It is three times the size of ours, and filled with the finest of everything. Aunt Martha has prepared the usual ham sandwiches with chips, pickles and a relish tray, applesauce with grated lemon, and devil's food cake with coffee icing. It's the usual meal, but nothing is "usual" at Aunt Martha's. Everything is special and arranged in beautiful ways.

We eat out in the breezeway, we visit for a bit, and then Mom gives some final words of encouragement to us. "I'm counting on you to be on your best behavior, and show Aunt Martha what wonderful little girls you are. Use your Sunday manners; you know how. Linda, Sharon is going to be with you the whole time, so you do not need to be afraid. I'm counting on you to be brave, O.K.? You're going to have a nice time." Linda's bottom lip is thick and quivering as they drive away, but she is very brave. Gently Uncle Clarence takes us by the hand, reminds us that he needs our help to go over to the Circus Store to pick up some cream soda for Aunt Martha and Pepsi for us.Thus, the adventure begins. Who is going to be the first one to sit on the armrest of the big green Buick? Sharon, of course.

## MONDAY, JULY 5

It's Monday on this Fourth of July weekend. We are spending the whole day at Miller Park celebrating. The zoo is open in the morning, so we watch the lion and tiger pacing in their cages for a while. They seem restless and bored, and very large. Are we really safe out here? We laugh at the monkeys swinging in their cages, picking little things out of each other's fur, and imitating the behavior of people watching. We rush over to see the peacock as other folks are telling us he has his feathers spread wide. We get there just in time to see his display. Wow! We have tried to see it before, but never have.

Having experienced that, we head over to the bandstand. The red-uniformed band is playing all of our favorite John Phillip Sousa patriotic marches. Afterward, Uncle Clarence takes us up onto the bandstand to meet the drummers. We are thrilled. When the twins used to come for visits as we are now, Uncle Clarence was actually one of the drummers; he still has his drum in the basement.

They have the amusement park rides going, so we ride the Merry-Go-Round more than once. It is a little scary for Linda, especially that little jiggle when it first starts. She holds tight to the bar as the horse goes up and down, wanting to wave to Aunt Martha and Uncle Clarence as we come around to where they are, but afraid to let go. Sharon is bouncing herself up and down on her horse and hanging dangerously to the side as she waves and waves.

**TUESDAY, JULY 6**

The joys of the celebration seemed to go on and on. Aunt Martha had filled the wooden picnic basket with fried chicken drumsticks, potato salad, and baked beans, and then served it on the tablecloth with the red cherries all over it. We were hungry and ate until we were stuffed. Lemonade from the big green thermos topped it off and helped us wash down the last of the chocolate cake with coffee icing.

After our meal, we rode the little steam engine train around the park. At the far side of the circle, we went through a little tunnel where the engineer never fails to blow the whistle (woooo,woooooo) causing a belch of smoke that smells the same every time. It has become a welcome smell, like an old friend. By the time the train ride was over, it was dark enough for the fireworks they set off at the lake. Uncle Clarence spread out the blanket on the hood of the car, hiking us up onto it, where we oo'd and ah'd until we were worn out and headed for "home".

**WEDNESDAY, JULY 7**

Ever since the celebration of the Fourth, we have been playing with our new cap guns that Uncle Clarence bought us with the red rolls of caps. We love that gunpowder smell when we shoot them. They

are still a little stiff when you pull the trigger, but
they will loosen up in time. We played with sparklers
tonight, too, once it was dark. We were careful, just
like Aunt Martha warned us, to stay back from each
other and not get them near our eyes. On the driveway
are countless round burn marks where we have been
lighting snake fireworks. They are fun to watch,
oozing and winding, gray ash snakes, slithering over
the ground.

## THURSDAY, JULY 8

Some time during the week, we always go to town
with Aunt Martha on the bus. We get dressed in nice
clean dresses, put on our Mary Jane's, and walk down
the block past the pretty white birch trees on the
corner, turn right, and at the next corner, we wait just
a moment or two before the big green bus arrives. We
hop on, deposit our tokens into the see-through box
by the driver's seat, pausing a moment to watch them
bump their way down like balls in the pinball machine
we have seen in the taverns in Wisconsin. The friendly
bus driver wants to know who Mrs. Jacobssen's
beautiful fellow travelers are today. "My sister's girls
visiting from Streator," she answers. "We are giving
their mother a little rest."

Up onto the seats we climb, and we bounce along,
our feet unable to reach the floor. Because we never
ride a bus at home, there is magic to it. How far it is
to go to town compared to at home where we walk four
blocks and are there! We whiz along block after block,
mile after mile. By the time we get to town, the empty
bus we entered is now full. Aunt Martha tells one of
us to pull the cord to tell the driver we want to get off
at the next stop. It feels very important to pull the

cord. We exit down the deep stairs with Aunt Martha
holding tightly to our hands. She doesn't want to lose
her sister's little treasures.

We have several errands to do before our favorite
store. First we stop at the drug store for a little lunch.
We sit on the chrome stools that twirl. Linda has to
kneel to reach the counter. Grill cheeses and chocolate
ice cream sodas are a treat. We like to watch the
waitress squirt the fizzy water into the tall soda glass.
We need two spoons and two straws, as one soda is
enough for the two of us.

After lunch, we go to the yarn shop to pick up some
supplies for Aunt Martha's needlepoint projects. She
works her needlepoint every night while we watch the
news and have our nightcap...we have Pepsi, Aunt
Martha and Uncle Clarence have a grown-up drink
that is light brown and has a cherry in it. After the
yarn shop, we need to stop by the little grocery store
to pick out a few things. The grocery boy will deliver
them in a cardboard box later in the day. That is
different than at home, too.

Finally we arrive at Rowland's Department Store,
our favorite stop. As we enter, we are greeted by
the heavenly fragrance of elegant cologne. Weaving
our way through the aisles of cashmere, cosmetics
and leather, we are greeted by numerous clerks who
clearly recognize their regular customer. The little
elevator man reminds us to watch our step, slides the
folding brass gate across, and we ascend to the toy
department on the second floor.

We pass display counters of stuffed animals, toy
airplanes, tin soldiers, and Lionel trains to the closed
glass cases containing the Madame Alexander dolls
and their never-ending clothing and accessories. It

is almost too much to take in all at once. There is
nothing in our realm of experience to compare with
it. While picking our favorites, we know we have just
come to look and dream. That is enough to satisfy us
for days.

Before catching the bus for home, we drop by the
funeral home to say "Hello" to Uncle Clarence. We are
always happy to go to the funeral home.

## JULY 9

No place on earth is as special as the Beck
Memorial Funeral Home! In the style of a large
red brick Southern mansion with white columns
surrounded by immaculately kept grounds, it is
magnificent, and our uncle owns it (partly owns it); he
is the undertaker. The driveway on the left, the one we
usually use, the one under the portico, has the hearse
(the special car made to carry caskets) parked there
and a long line of elegant cars behind it. That means
they are having a funeral right now, and are ready
for the solemn funeral procession to the cemetery.
We have to be extra quiet and respectful. We step
out of the world and into the hushed atmosphere of
this elegant "Home." Stepping gently on the plush
red carpet, we hear Westminster chimes somewhere
down the hall. It is very chilly inside, and there is an
overwhelming fragrance of gladiolas and roses. Today
there are many, many huge beautiful bouquets. "Why
do people buy flowers for dead people?" we wonder.
"They can't smell them anymore." If we were dead, we
would surely like to go to such a beautiful place and
have our loved ones say very quietly that we were good
and kind, helpful and energetic, sensitive and loving...
and playful. Uncle Clarence, in his gray pinstriped

three-piece suit, stands at the door, looking very kind
and caring, slightly bent forward in concern.

When there is a viewing time, if we are there, we
often stroll through the chapel and see the body. We've
seen them many times. They look kind of yellow, with
a little bit of grey around their mouth, and they never
smile. We know we have pretty smiles, so we don't
want to be dead quite yet. They also have their hands
folded sweetly on their chest. When we play hide and
seek down in the casket room, sometimes we practice
being still like dead people so no one will find us,
folding our hands just so. It's kind of fun. The caskets
are just like rolling beds, like grown-up basinets.

**JULY 10**

Aunt Martha does the dead people's hair, nails
and make-up. She's their beautician, and even wears
pearly blue eye shadow herself. Our mom never does
that, but she wears powder and lipstick. In Aunt
Martha's closet, she has a whole row of formals, too.
Our mom doesn't even have one, because she never
goes to a ball. One day Aunt Martha was going to do
the make-up of a lady that had been her friend; she
wanted her to look just right, "like she had just gone
to sleep," she explained. Sharry thought that was
strange to put make-up on for going to sleep. Our
Mom always took hers off before going to bed.

*If that dead person knew what we were doing,*
*they would roll over in their grave.*

**JULY 11**

I, Sharry, know all about what they do to dead
people, so I have to explain everything to Linda. Big

sisters always have to teach their little sisters the things they have learned. There is a smell in the funeral home and in the embalming room. It's the smell of the embalming fluid. You can't really smell it when there are so many flowers around, but when they aren't there, you can. It's not a bad smell; I kind of like it.

What they do is, first they drain all of the blood out of the body. Don't worry, it doesn't hurt them because they are dead and can't feel it. Then they put in the embalming fluid. That way the body keeps a lot longer. The bodies keep longer in the cold, too, which is why the funeral home is always so cold, so we have to wear our sweaters and not just our sundresses when we go there.

## JULY 12

In the basement, next to the casket room, is the smoking lounge. We hate all the smoke down there because it makes us choke, but in that room is a magical red cola machine. Mostly men hang out in this small den. They are getting away from the crying women. The men are always kind to us because they know we belong to Uncle Clarence. They buy us each a cola in a green bottle. After our cola, we visit Uncle Clarence's office. We know just which one it is, down the hall, in the corner on the right. On the wall is a lovely soft green painting with a poem in the middle that starts out, "I think that I shall never see A poem lovely as a tree" and ends with "Poems are made by fools like me, But only God can make a tree." Usually Uncle Clarence has to finish up some "unfinished business" as he calls it. We wait quietly on his chairs with our hands folded in our lap. That is when we gaze at the pretty picture with the poem.

When Uncle Clarence finishes up, he gives us a
ride home in the big green Buick. It's Linda's turn to
be on the armrest in the middle of the front seat. It's a
smooth ride compared to riding in our Chevrolet.

[This was in the days before seat belts.]

**JULY 13**

Aunt Martha is working at the Park Presbyterian
Church today preparing food with the other ladies
for a luncheon. Linda is along, too. The ladies are
cooking chickens for chicken salad. The fragrance of
chickens cooking fills the air. The ladies are all chatty
and laughing, teasing each other. As a little observer,
I, Linda, think to myself, " Protestant ladies have so
much more fun than Catholic ladies. We never do this
sort of thing. It's too bad we're Catholics. Oh well."

While we did that, Sharry went to the dentist with
Uncle Clarence. She can't go to the dentist at home
because she had a fit and kicked his chair, so he won't
let her come back. Uncle Clarence's dentist is nicer
anyway. After the dentist, they went to the American
Legion Hall for fried chicken and watermelon. What
fun!

**JULY 14**

Today is the day the Santa Fe passenger train
comes through, so we are excited to see it. At the
station, Uncle Clarence boosts us up onto the wooden
luggage cart, so we can see better. We can hear the
whistle of the train while it is still a long way off.
We hear it blow at every crossing, getting closer and
closer, making us more and more excited.

Finally it arrives, black engine blowing off steam and smoke, filling the air, immense wheels rolling and rolling, steel on steel, so loud we can't even talk, and finally screeching to a stop. People get off and people get on. "All abooooard," the porter yells out, pulling up the little step stool. The train eases out of the station and is gone. How we love it when Uncle Clarence takes us to the train station!

**JULY 15**

This night is one of our favorite nights. It is the ice cream social at church. We have just a light supper so we will have plenty of room for dessert. Cars are parked solid for blocks around. Everyone loves an ice cream social! As the sun sets, we see the tables all set up outside in the churchyard, lit up by strings of lights. One big table is for pies, all homemade, every kind you can imagine, apple and cherry and blueberry with fancy sugary crusts, and some with only one crust: banana cream, lemon meringue, and pecan, even pumpkin, though it isn't Thanksgiving. There are thick peach pies with crumb topping and strawberry rhubarb, all juicy and pink.

A second table holds the cakes, all homemade, in many colors and flavors: large round chocolate layer cakes on beautiful raised stands and white cakes with fluffy white frosting are in the back, with marble cakes, and German chocolate cakes with the coconut frosting closer to the front. The angel food cake sits next to a huge bowl of strawberries and whipped cream. How will we ever decide which to choose? Gentlemen in white aprons are scooping out vanilla, strawberry, and chocolate ice cream from large brown paper barrels.

Our tickets are bent and moist from being held
in our hands while we survey this wondrous sight.
This again is far beyond anything we have ever
experienced. Sharon chooses the biggest piece of
chocolate cake, with chocolate ice cream, of course,
and Linnie just can't decide, so she gets the same
thing as Uncle Clarence, cherry pie a la mode. The
night air is cool and dark. The lightening bugs are
out. Mouths and hands are sticky, and faces are full of
smiles...our tummies are full, too.

**JULY 16**

Early this morning, we snuck downstairs, as we
often do, and peaked into Uncle Clarence's bathroom
when he was shaving. Even before we looked in, we
smelled the familiar scent of his sandalwood soap
and shaving cream. How funny he looked in his long
blue pajamas, with no glasses and mussed up hair, so
different than the way he usually looks in his three-
piece suit. He looked like a clown preparing for the
circus. We watched, spellbound, as he methodically
spread the shaving cream on cheeks and chin,
carefully around his mouth, and down his neck.

We didn't think he knew we were there, though
we couldn't help giggling a little bit at how funny he
looked. And then, surprise! He put a dab right at
the end of his nose, and turned to see us straight on.
We all burst into laughter. He knew we were there
after all. It was always the same game, but always a
surprise.

Looking rather sheepish, Linda then whispered
into Uncle Clarence's ear that she had a secret to
share with him. Gently he listened to the dilemma.
Yesterday, while getting a drink of water, the little

frosted glass had slipped out of her hand and broken on the kitchen floor. Quickly she had hidden it in the bushes out front before Aunt Martha had noticed.

"Don't you worry any more about this," Uncle Clarence assured her. "I'll take care of everything, and I won't let the cat out of the bag. Aunt Martha will never know." Linnie sighed a big sigh of relief, and it was never mentioned again.

*Don't spill the beans! Don't let the cat out of the bag!*

## JULY 17

It is a sad day for Sharry, for we had to come back home. She would have liked to stay forever with Aunt Martha and Uncle Clarence. Of course, she couldn't do that, but she always wishes she could. It doesn't seem fair. In the car, she was filled with dread; back home her anger and frustration boiled just below the surface. In Bloomington, she was the star, and it was easy to be an angel. At home, where she has to share the stage, things get all complicated.

It made it all the worse that Linda's reaction was just the opposite. Linda is very glad to be back home. Home, where you don't have to always use your best manners, and you can wear your dirty socks to bed if your feet are cold, where the sheets are soft because they are kind of worn out, and the towels are thin enough to dry your ears. Home, where if you break a glass, you don't have to keep it a secret, you just have to clean up the mess, and home, with the comfort of your Mother always near at hand.

*You always want what you can not have,*
*and that is not good.*

— 227 —

**JULY 18**

We are not the only two that have been gone. Marcia was chosen to represent the saxophone section of the band at band camp in DuQoin, so she was gone all week, too. She went with Nancy, who played the clarinet, and Tom who played the trombone. They had a great time! The band sang with the chorus as well, and that was a real change for her. Marilyn and Linda are the ones who always sing in choruses, while Marcia and Sharon are in the band. At camp, they sang "Ole Buttermilk Sky" and "Rock a my Soul in the Bosom of Abraham", so she experienced the joy of four part harmony.

**JULY 19**

From fifth grade on, Marcia loves spending time with the band. Activities include her own personal practices and private lessons, learning marching band routines, band practices, playing gigs at dances and sock hops, performing with the jazz band wearing their "jazzy" maroon corduroy blazers with black ties, and putting on concerts, of course.

She is one of only two girls chosen to be in the jazz band. Before this year, the jazz band was strictly boys, but this year they were short on boys, so they let in a couple of girls. Fooling around in the band room is a lot more fun than study hall, so that's where you can find her every morning, enjoying the camaraderie, and helping to organize the uniforms and other band paraphernalia. This is her own world, apart from her life as a twin and a sister and a daughter. That makes it extra special.

## JULY 20

Marilyn was not very thrilled to be the one to have
to stay home to work at the store last week, but she's
the practical one, always willing to do what needs to
be done. Besides, she got the bedroom and the bed
and the bathroom mirror all to herself. That was
a real luxury! With four girls, plus Mom, and one
bathroom, we sometimes have three or four of us using
it at the same time, one at the mirror, one on the John,
and one in the tub. We have never had a shower. Our
neighbor Matt Hamilton put one in their basement,
but none of us have ever had a shower, so we see no
need. The tub works fine. Besides, our dad just doesn't
do handy-man jobs.

## JULY 21

The days are pretty warm now, so Linda is
assigned the task of checking the little box on the
front porch to see if the yellow milk truck from Illinois
Valley Dairy has delivered the milk yet. We want to
make sure we get the bottles in from the porch in good
time before the milk spoils.

While she was waiting for the truck, she heard the
bell of the scissor man, a gypsy peddler who strolls the
streets in summer and offers to sharpen your knives
and scissors. He is quite a colorful character, with
a crushed felt hat, baggy clothes, and a pack on his
back that holds his sharpening tools. We didn't need
anything sharpened this time, so he just moved on,
ringing his bell.

**JULY 22**

Marcia tried on five outfits this morning, trying to decide what to wear. Then she left all five of them on the end of their bed. Sharon was fit to be tied. She has been cranky ever since we got home anyway. Seems like every day she gets up on the wrong side of the bed, but that was the last straw. "Get these things out of my way!" she yelled at Marcia. Marcia had stretched the phone into the bathroom to talk in private, and was not moving fast enough for Sharon's satisfaction. Next thing we knew Sharon had tossed them all down the clothes chute. Now Marcia will be looking for them one of these days and find them in the basement. It is a very small house for us some days.

*Did you get up on the wrong side of the bed today?*

**JULY 23**

The lightning bugs were really out tonight. We caught a whole bunch, putting them in jars with lids. Then we pulled off their lights, stuck them together and made rings. They glow in the dark for a pretty long time even though they are no longer attached to the bugs. It's really neat. Unfortunately, the mosquitoes were out, too, so we were covered with bites, and were quite miserable with all of the scratching. By the time Mom put pink Calamine lotion on all of them, we were looking quite polka-dotted everywhere.

[We are horrified when we look back on how insensitive we were toward these poor innocent harmless bugs, but times were different then.]

## JULY 24

Day after day this summer, little Linnie is begging Sharry to please, please teach her to draw a five-point star. "Twinkle, twinkle little star, I wish that I could draw a star," was what she said at night when the stars came out. Big sisters have so many things to teach their little sisters! Sharry was eager to teach her, but the time had to be just right.

Today was just the right day. There was so much excitement in it. Pencils ready, here we go. " Up on one, and down on two, to make an upside down V, then across and up on three, and straight across on four, then back all the way to the start on five. One, two, three, four, five. She demonstrated several more times. "Now you try. You can do it! Don't worry about how they look. We can fix it later," Sharry encouraged. Linnie tried and tried again, and each one looked better than the one before. One, two, three, four, five. One, two, three, four, five. "I'll be right back," Sharry said, and was gone. Linnie kept practicing. " This isn't as hard as I thought," she was thinking to herself. "Glitter!" Sharry yelled as she burst back into the room. "Mom gave me glitter so we can make your stars shine!" That was the perfect ending to a perfect sister learning time.

Here is how we wish on a star, the first one you see at night: *"Star light, Star bright, First star I see tonight. I wish I may; I wish I might, have the wish I wish tonight."* Then make a wish, and it's done.

*You never know until you try.*

## JULY 25

July is always the month for travel. One year (1956), Sharon, Linda, and cousin Judy are invited to accompany Aunt Millie and Uncle Jeff on a trip to Denver, Colorado to visit our Aunt Pauline. We have never been on a really big trip before, and have never seen true mountains. We consider the slack piles over near Wenona , one hundred feet high or so, to be the highest mountains we have seen so far.

## JULY 26

Hour after hour, day after day, we drive through cornfields and grasslands and rolling hills, through towns and cities, and finally through wide open spaces, where we see tumbleweed for the first time blowing along the ground. In Kansas, we stop to see Dodge City, the real Dodge City portrayed on the TV program Gunsmoke, including the Boot Hill Cemetery, and the saloon, where we have a sassafras (old time root beer) to drink. The whole trip we are hot and sweaty, but Kansas is the worst. [This was before AC in cars.]

At long last, we see a purple fringe along the horizon. Those are the mountains Aunt Millie has praised so highly through the years. They don't look like much. When we drive up into them, days later, our opinion of them changes dramatically. They are much, much larger than we could ever have imagined, and much more beautiful. We note that as Uncle Jeff drives through them, Aunt Millie is constantly praying her rosary, and around the curves will frequently say, "Oh, Jesus, Mary and Joseph!" The constant heat that has plagued us the whole trip has turned to cool mountain air.

[Little did Linda know that someday she would live all of her adult life in those very same mountains.]

## JULY 27

The week has been full of sight seeing. We've seen Buffalo Bill's grave, the Mother Cabrini Shrine, the Garden of the Gods, Pike's Peak, the Denver Zoo, and (our favorite) an outdoor performance of the musical "Oklahoma!" in Cheeseman Park. It's been a busy week!

## JULY 28

Aunt Pauline is very swanky; she has real style! Her son, Steve (sometimes called "Junior") is our cousin, but it's funny, because he is already grown up, so he seems more like an uncle. We went to visit Steve and his wife Ruie in their beautiful fancy home. His band came over for a jam session, and Steve played the drums. I think maybe he isn't such a good person. He tells dirty jokes, which isn't very nice because we are just children.

Their daughter Chrissy has a doll that is homely, homely in a dear sort of way. Her name is Pitiful Pearl. Linda wishes she could have one just like it. They have a faucet in their kitchen sink with just one handle in the middle that controls turning the water off and on and whether it is hot or cold. We have never seen such a thing before.

Steve's wife Ruie is very beautiful. She gave Linda, a black two-piece swimsuit and some sort of falsies to push up her little starts of breasts. Mom will never let her wear such a thing in public, but it is kind of fun to play in and pretend she's all grown up. She is only ten years old. The trip home is even longer, but fortunately, we have many things to talk about.

[Later on, Linda and Ruie became very dear friends.]

**JULY 29**

[Marcia and Marilyn took almost the same trip with Aunt Millie and Uncle Jeff back in July 1950. Their recollections are very similar. Two years later they were taken on a sightseeing trip to the Northeast, New York City, and all the way up into Canada. How fortunate we were for our aunt and uncle to want to share the rich experience of travel with us, for our father was a stay-at-home guy. Except for crossing the border of Illinois up into Wisconsin for our summer vacations, and one trip that he took with Mom and the Harts up to Mackinaw, Michigan late in life, he never left his home state, and rarely left his hometown. In fact, he was born and raised in one house, married and moved to a house three doors down, and worked his whole life in a store four blocks away from that.

[Mom had traveled as a young woman, and loved it, but she waited to do more of it until after he died.]

**JULY 30**

Preparations began today for the annual vacation to Lake Delevan, Wisconsin. All of the clothes are washed but not ironed. Mom is making lists of food items and toiletries, linens and cleaning supplies to bring. Some things she is already packing in boxes to go on the trip.

**FRIDAY, JULY 31**

Dad likes to go to Wisconsin a great deal more than Mom. It's so much extra work for her. We leave tomorrow for a week. Mom has Marilyn ironing all of the clothes we will take. The rest of us girls walk to town with her to get the extra groceries we will take with us. We can all help carry the bags.

We haven't worn our swimming suits since last year for we don't have a pool in our town except the YMCA, and we have not taken any swim lessons at the "Y" this year. Linda has grown so much that her suit can barely still be worn. It's too short, and the elastic is worn out but there's no time now to shop for a new one, so it will have to do. The swim caps, nose clips, and blue rubber inner tube were miraculously all in the same box in the basement. Guess we'll be ready to leave in the morning.

*Sometimes we just have to make do*
*with what we have.*

*Bloomington Illinois*

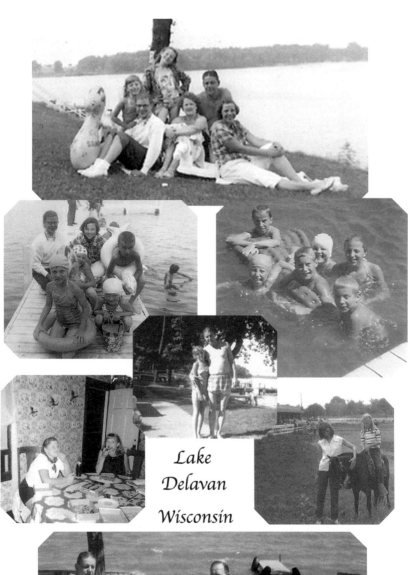

Lake
Delavan

Wisconsin

# Chapter Twelve — Any August
## Beating the Heat

SATURDAY   AUG. 1

Dad puts all the things Mom has packed into the trunk of the car, and we head north to Wisconsin, stopping in Hebron to see our cousins who sometimes go with us to Lake Geneva, but not this year. This year, for the umpteenth time, we are going to Lake Delavan to share the Brewster cottage with our closest friends,  Ralph and Eleanor Hart, who have a boy, Mal, a little older than we are and a girl, Kristy, a little younger. We can hardly wait to get there.

Brewster's is just up the hill from the water, and is pretty comfortable compared to some of the places we have stayed, especially the ones that did not have indoor plumbing. None of the cottages we rented are clean enough for Mom's standards, though, so the first thing she does when we arrive is clean, especially the bathrooms and kitchen, for who knows what sort of people were there the week before? She also has to make up the beds with the sheets we brought from home.

While Mom is doing that, Eleanor the sun-worshiper, having donned her swimsuit first thing, takes charge of the beach detail, gathering up the abundance of paraphernalia needed, including inner tubes, beach ball, beach towels, swim caps, nose plugs, webbed aluminum folding chairs, shovels and pails for sandcastle building, and suntan lotion, distributing them among the children, who are all bouncing up and down with excitement. Off we go, eager for the first plunge. Mom will eventually make it down to the water, dressed in one of her cotton sundresses. She'll sit in the shade, enjoying watching our antics in the water, happy to be settled in.

**SUNDAY AUG. 2**

Already by the end of today, Sharon, with her red hair and freckled white skin that never tans though slathered with Coppertone, having spent many hours at the lake in and out of the water, in spite of countless warnings about being in the sun too long, is terribly sunburned and will have to wear a T-shirt over her swimsuit the rest of the week.

**MONDAY AUG. 3**

We spend most of our time at the beach, not much of a beach, really, just two giant steps of sand, and then the squishy mud and slippery-rock bed of the lake, so uncomfortable upon entry that we use the ladder of the pier instead, though its mossy bottom is a bit creepy to us as well, or, better yet, just jump or dive right in off the pier. We don't see fish or go fishing,

but that fishy smell is everywhere, one of those smells
that makes Marilyn, particularly sensitive to smells,
scrunch up her nose. She also smells the dishrag every
time before using it.

## TUESDAY AUG. 4

While we are in the water or on the pier, Dad is
in a little tavern, just a stone's throw from the water.
Another larger one is at the top of the hill. Because
we go to the same place year after year, he is pretty
good friends with the bartenders. We can overhear
them talking baseball as the televised game goes
on indefinitely, hour after hour, with an occasional
roar as a home run is finally hit. We run in and out
during the day for some pop or pretzels or beer nuts,
in partial blindness, moving from the bright light
and heat of the sun into the cool dark recesses of the
tavern, lit only by the "sky blue waters" sign across
the back wall, toward the familiar silhouette of our
dad at the bar, a ribbon of gray smoke coming up from
the red tip of his cigarette, that dank, boozy, stale beer
smell as familiar to us as it was to our father growing
up in his father's saloon. He is relaxed and congenial,
a different father than the one we know at home, the
one weighed down by the burdens of his business and
by the trends he sees in the culture around him as he
reads the paper at the table each night, the one who
says little, but often sighs.

## WEDNESDAY AUG. 5

Around mealtimes, we are drawn into the tavern,
too. Taverns make the best food, our favorites being
fried chicken, spaghetti with meatballs, Italian beef
sandwiches and cheeseburgers, offering us, and Mom,

a break from the rest of the meals that she prepares
in the cottage using unfamiliar cooking tools and less
than ideal pans served on mismatched dishes, food we
eat with forks with bent tines and spoons that have
been used to pry things open.

[It should be noted that at this time in the history
of our country there are still no fast food chains. No
McDonald's, No Arby's, No Pizza Huts, No KFC.]

**THURSDAY AUG. 6**

We have had such good weather all week that
we are all rather parched, but today it rained all
morning, perfect for working on our puzzle, for being
lazy, and for peeling the blistered skin off of our
shoulders and backs.

This afternoon, it cleared up, so we went to town,
walking through souvenir shops, wanting to buy
everything we saw, but contenting ourselves with
munching on fresh Karmelcorn and licking drippy ice
cream cones. Mom says we don't need any more cedar
chest boxes, tom tom drums made of birch bark or
Indian headdresses.

**FRIDAY AUG. 7**

Every evening, the grown-ups play Canasta, the
same way they play cards on Saturday nights at home.
The whoops and hollers of elation and disappointment
increase in intensity as the evening wears on, as
cards are won and lost, as more beer is consumed,
and especially as the pile is frozen, getting larger and
larger, finally being captured by someone, ensuring a
win.

Enjoying staying up late night after night, we kids

play our own card games, usually Hearts, trying to
keep from getting any hearts or the queen of spades,
until some sneaky person "shoots the moon," ending
the evening with groans as everyone else loses.
Tomorrow we go home already. These weeks always go
by very fast.

*Where does the time go?*

SATURDAY AUG. 8

Pack up, clean up, and home we go. Before we leave,
for the perfect ending to our week, Mrs. Brewster, the
nice lady who owns our cabin, brings us some of her
special Scandinavian rosettes, a fried cookie coated
with powdered sugar. We are sandy, sunburned,
and worn out, but happy. Mom is just plain worn
out. Perhaps, she's thinking of how she is going to
have to unpack everything when we get home, wash
everything, and find some way to get the sand out of
every pocket and particle of everything we own. Dad
doesn't say anything as he drives home, but he does
have a hint of a smile.

SUNDAY AUG. 9

It's really hard to be back home! It would be much
better to live right on a lake like the kids we met in
Wisconsin, those lucky teenage girls who wash their
hair in the lake, which seems so glamorous. It's cooler
there, too. Here, it is unbearably hot, and humid.

Mom said we should count our blessings and not
complain anymore, reminding us that our Madame
Alexander dolls are probably feeling pretty lonely and
neglected since we have been gone so long. She was
right. They were very glad to see us take them out

of their cases, especially when we had them go on a
vacation to a lake in Wisconsin and to the mountains
of Colorado, so we all had a lot of fun.

**MONDAY AUG. 10**
 It was already hot when we woke up this morning.
Mom said it was going to be a real scorcher, and it
was! That made everyone kind of crabby. No one had
to help with the dishes tonight because we all said
it was someone else's turn, so Mom said she'd rather
just do it herself than hear us bicker. It was really
Sharon's turn, but she wouldn't admit it.

[After we were all through college and on our own,
Mom finally had air conditioning put in. Dad had died
in 1965.]

**TUESDAY AUG. 11**
 Because it was so hot again, Mom encouraged us to
go down to play in the basement, since it's cooler down
there. She said if we were busy, the time would pass a
lot more quickly. There is plenty to keep us occupied
down there. We read musty old comics for a long time,
digging into the two feet high stack. Our favorite is
Little Lulu, who, incidentally, is fun to draw, with the
two circle curls up on top, banana curls framing the
sides of her peanut shaped head, and a little upside-
down "v" for a nose.
 Next we decided to play house. We keep our house
set up with the wooden table and chairs on a nice
old rug. Around the edge of this area is a waist-high
cement slab that makes a perfect countertop where
we have a little metal toy stove with a set of copper-
bottomed pans, including a tea kettle, a small sink,

and a pink diaper pail, which we pretend is a washing machine. Using the same china tea set that the twins played with when they were our age, we had a tea party.

We don't bring our good Madame Alexander dolls down there because they might get dirty since the coal bin is right on the other side of the furnace, but everyone else was there, all of the old rubber dolls and a couple of teddy bears. Overhead are the clotheslines Mom uses in the winter, but they did not get in our way because we aren't that tall. After playing house, we worked on some old mimeograph sheets that were too easy for us, but we like to do the easy ones sometimes just for fun. It makes us feel extra smart. Before we knew it, this hot day was past.

[Somewhere along the way, the coal furnace was changed to an oil furnace, so we no longer had coal delivered to the coal bin. The year Dad was so sick with cancer so that she had to frequently change the sheets, Mom finally insisted that they get a clothes dryer. That was 1964.]

**WEDNESDAY AUG. 12**

What a long day! About half of it, we just sat on the porch watching people go by, wishing we had something fun to do, too hot to think of anything. Brenda Holbrook and the Samek triplets walked by, and big old Mr. Buck, dressed in his usual brown pants and shirt, pedaled slowly by on his brown bicycle, all heading North to town and then South again like yoyo's returning to the top of their strings. We counted cars going by for a while, but they were few and far between.

It feels like it could rain; it's so humid, but then it doesn't. It weighs us down so we can hardly breathe. Marcia and Marilyn are helping at the store, but there's probably not much business since it's much too hot to shop. The final Summer Weekly Readers came today so that helped a little, but this summer has gotten way too hot and way too long.

**THURSDAY AUG. 13**

In spite of the heat, we are starting to think of school again, now just two weeks away. Except for Christmas, these are the longest two weeks of the year. "Back to School" sales are going on, so we dug out our school clothes from last year to see what fits and if we need anything. Linda was able to fit into some of Sharon's dresses from last year, ones she has eagerly been waiting for, and a few others that definitely looked better on Sharry than they do on her. Sharry is so hard on her clothes that some of them just had to be pitched. Sadly, we have outgrown some of our favorite things.

**FRIDAY AUG. 14**

Mom's nose was itching today, so she said that always means we must be going to get company. That would be pretty amazing since we never get company. Well, almost never.

Marcia helped Mom wash the white metal Venetian blinds from all six windows today, the living room and the bedrooms. Sitting out in the yard most of the day with a bucket of Spic and Span water, they remove every slat, wash, dry, put it back, and clip it in place. Then the windows get washed and the blinds are hung back up, a long and tedious job, but they enjoy the

time together, chatting about this, that and the other.
[Years later, Linda helped her with this, and it was
pleasurable as well.]

There are two conflicting styles of working in our
family, this being the perfect example of one of them.
It is "If we have to do a job, we may as well just take
our time, and enjoy it." Mom, Marcia, and Linda have
this philosophy, while Marilyn and Sharon think just
the opposite: "If we have to do this job, let's do it as
fast as we can and get it over with, so we can go on
and do something we enjoy." Sharon cuts the grass
each Saturday with the push mower. That's more her
style. It's a good thing we are all different; that way
all of the jobs get done.


SATURDAY    AUG. 15

Saturday is bath and shampoo day at our house
since Mom wants us to be clean and pretty for church
on Sunday. For years, all of our little shoes were
polished on Saturday as well. In the new kitchen,
Mom lays the younger girls down on the counter, gets
out the Lustre Crème shampoo and Tame cream rinse,
and washes our hair over the kitchen sink where
she is able to rinse it with our fancy new sprayer
built right into the sink. Though we have a tub, it
seems like Dad only takes sponge baths at the little
bathroom sink that is the size of a large bowl, but he
is always meticulously clean, and has the soft hands
and clean fingernails of a businessman.


[Until 1949, we had an indoor toilet, but not an
actual bathroom. A metal tub was brought up from the

basement into the center of the kitchen where heated water and hot water from the kitchen sink were added. Each child was bathed in turn. After our bath, we were sprinkled with April Showers talcum powder, especially in summer when it was hard to get dry because of the humidity, which helped us avoid getting prickly heat rash, a fairly common problem. After the bathroom was added where the back porch had been, bathing was much easier, but we still stuck to the Saturday schedule. Bathing was more frequent in the summer, especially if we got sweaty or if our feet were filthy from going barefoot, which they often were.]

### SUNDAY AUG. 16

No roast today, for the kitchen was sweltering even without the oven being on. Mom said it was too hot to cook, but we talked her into making us fried chicken anyway. We all love it, so the pieces disappeared in no time. By the time Mom sat down, the only thing left was the back. Mom said it was ok, because her favorite piece was always the back... and the neck. She said her mother always made soup out of the neck, and it was delicious.

[Later in her life, after we were grown, she often went out for fried chicken. She never ordered the back or the neck.]

### MONDAY AUG. 17

Maybe there is something true about that saying when your nose is itching, for Aunt Bee came up to visit us from Bloomington today. She never did that before. She arrived in the afternoon right at the end of the baseball game, so we turned the TV off and don't

know who won because Mom thinks it is rude to watch
television if someone comes to visit. Uncle Clarence
watches the news when we go to visit him, but I guess
that's different. Aunt Bee says it is just as hot in
Bloomington as it is here. With two of us in each of
the three beds at our house, our bedrooms are full, so
Aunt Bee will sleep on the couch.

**TUESDAY AUG. 18**
 Aunt Bee just stayed one night, but what fun we
had! She was such a jolly good sport, we laughed and
laughed. It was so hot, that we couldn't sleep in our
stuffy bedroom where there wasn't a breath of air, so
Mom let us spread comforters and blankets on the
floor of the living room, cover them with sheets, and
sleep there, us on the floor and Aunt Bee on the couch,
with the front door open on one end and the kitchen
windows open in the back, the screen door allowing us
to get a little breeze flowing through. Finally we were
comfortable enough to sleep, after we got over all the
giggles, that is.

[Aunt Bee only visited us that one time.]


**WEDNESDAY AUG. 19**
 There is no let-up on the heat; the aggravation
is getting to us. Marcia and Sharon got into an
argument about some dumb thing today. Fortunately
Marilyn, our peacemaker, intervened with a message
that Mom was ready for Marcia to hang the clothes
out on the line. She also reminded Sharon that she
hasn't read her favorite book "Misty" yet this summer
and, it's already August, so she better get to it. Linda

was off in her own world reading a Cherry Ames book, dreaming of being a strong heroic nurse someday, which inspired her to play student nurse in her blue striped apron with a white paper cap on her head, bandaging up everyone in sight. Ever since her eye infection when she was six, she has been anemic, so she dreams of being strong, and of being a nurse, like her nurse in the hospital, Donna Gallick, who was so kind and helpful.* Marilyn's task today was washing everything from the china cabinet, but Mom came to put the things away herself, just the way she wants them. "There," she said, "that is the final cleaning job of the summer. What a great feeling that is."

*[Linda eventually received a Bachelor of Science in Nursing from Loyola University. She enjoyed working as a registered nurse a good number of years.]

THURSDAY AUG. 20

In the morning, it wasn't too hot yet, so we decided to jump rope*, only we couldn't find a third person to help twirl until Marcia came home from the library and twirled for us. Sharon got hot pepper over a hundred, disappointing to her because she wanted to get to a hundred and fifty, while Linda got over thirty-five which is good for her. She was happy the rest of the day.

Good thing we jumped rope early, for later on it was beastly hot, making us so lethargic we ended up falling asleep, but when we woke up everyone was in an even worse mood. Sharon was fit to be tied, fuming and smoldering. We have to stay out of her way.

*[See jump rope rhymes in Appendix D]

**FRIDAY AUG. 21**

Today was just like yesterday and the day before and the day before, *hot, humid* and *boring!* And we don't want to play in the basement. On top of everything else, there is a pukey smell in the air today, the smell of silage left over from canning corn at the Canning Factory, rotting in the heat. Even though the canning factory is only a couple of blocks away, we hardly ever smell it. That sure is *not* true today! The wind must be coming from the South. Maybe that South wind will bring in the welcome relief of a storm. A little over a week and we can go back to school. Can we make it through this *last* week?

[At least one year, Uncle Albert worked at the Canning Factory. How did he *do* it? Effluent from the factory sometimes made its way into the creek, which flowed nearby. No wonder it was called the "Stink Creek", pronounced, "crick". Summer storms brought the threat of tornadoes, but we still longed for them to relieve us from the oppressive humidity.]

**SATURDAY AUG. 22**

In the morning, before it was too hot, we walked to town to have our physicals for school. Our doctor's name is "D.O.Conley", so his initials spell DOC. Isn't that cool? Today, we get to see if our "tickers" are still working properly. That is what he calls listening to our hearts. We love going to see Dr. Conley except for two things: getting our vaccinations and surviving Mildred, the receptionist, a no-nonsense person, who expects our behavior to be perfect. We aren't even to say a word. We try, but after a while, we are quite antsy, want so badly to leave our seats, and need to talk, at least a little bit. Mildred reminds us that we have to stay quietly seated until called. We swing our legs under the chairs just for something to do, but a frown and slight shake of Mom's head tells us that that is not appropriate, either.

Finally we are called, and the three of us go in together to see the doctor. We are measured and weighed, hold the glass thermometer under our tongues for the longest time, and then Linnie crawls up on Mom's lap, letting Sharry go first. Sharry tries to be a brave big sister and do just what the doctor orders. He is easy to please, very kind and lovable, even jolly. With his plump body planted firmly on a little stool, he gently pulls her into the safe space, right before him. He checks out her "ticker", putting the cold stethoscope on her bare chest. "Good as ever," he says. After Linda gets the same treatment, and the records are filled out, we go to Hills Brothers for a little treat.

Here are a few good health tips:
1 - *Don't pick your nose; you'll make it bleed.*
2 - *Don't pick your scab or you'll get it infected and end up with a scar.*
3 - *Booboos always feel better if you kiss them.*

**SUNDAY AUG. 23**

A vignette by Linda:   A couple of kids were playing with matches over behind Counselman's garage on this warm night. We had had a game of Kick the Can in the alley and everyone had drifted away, but I was drawn over to see what these kids were doing. I knew better than to play with fire, but this wasn't really

fire, it was just matches. They asked if I had ever lit
a match before, and I hadn't. I wanted to be like the
big kids, so I said I would like to. About that time,
Sharry came by and saw what I was doing. She told
me I was in really big trouble, and, that I would get
a big spanking for sure. I thought maybe I would just
run away. I could go about as far as Gregory Stanton's
house in the next block, but then I didn't know after
that. Maybe they would take me in. Then Sharry came
and told me that Mom wouldn't spank me if I came
home, so I decided not to run away after all.

As it turned out, when I came home, Mom said if I
was playing with fire she would have to give me "the
switch". So we got a flexible little branch off of one
of the bushes outside and she gave me a few flicks of
that on my bottom and the top of my legs. It stung
pretty badly, but the worst part was the sting of
betrayal. Sharry told me she wasn't going to give me
"the switch", but she *did*! I never played with matches
again, but I felt betrayed for a long time. That was the
first and last spanking I ever remember.

## AUG. 24

Sharry speaks out:  The heat, the summer idleness,
the inactivity, it's all getting to me. It's so hot the birds
aren't even singing. Even Marilyn and Linda, who are
usually at least humming something, aren't singing
either. I'm stripped down to next to nothing, but I'm
still burning up. My head is pounding, too. That's
what this horrible heat does to me, weighing me down,
pulling my hair, crushing my chest, and making me
nauseated. If I were just bored, I could eat, but not
now. I can't even *think!* Ants are crawling on my legs
and I'm too hot to even brush them away.

I'm trapped, exhausted. It's like the sun becomes this horrible *monster* that strips me, leaving me all used up, crushing me so that I can hardly breathe. I hate the sun monster! My sisters have gone somewhere. Where are they? I don't know. I'm all alone. I'm stinging everywhere, on my legs, on my bottom. There is my Dad, belt in hand, yelling at me to stop screaming, lashing out, again and again. I defy him again and again. I won't cry. I won't give in no matter how hard he hits me. I won't. I won't. I won't. "Help me!" I cry out, but no one comes. In the nightmare no one comes. I wake up exhausted. The sun monster has gotten me again.

[This recurring nightmare came as a result of an incident that occurred earlier in Sharry's life, when her dad really beat her. Though she was often in trouble due to her sassy mouth, this only happened once, and none of us knows what Sharry could have done to aggravate Dad enough to cause such drastic action; perhaps he had been drinking. Maybe that last act or word of rebellion was just the last straw, the straw that broke the camel's back, or maybe the sun monster got him, too. Linda and Mom watched, frozen in silence, horrified. The next day, life went on as usual.]

*Life goes on. Time heals all wounds.*

**AUG. 25**

There is really nothing to cure the misery we are all suffering from except to have summer over and a new year begin. So we just pick up our chins and move on. We love having our mother home for the summer, and we always look forward to summer vacations, but then we can't wait for school to start. After she finished up the supper dishes tonight, Mom sat down with a sigh. "I'll be glad to be back to school, back in the old routines. It will be good for us all."

## AUG. 26

Mom says we can get a couple new dresses to start out the year right, but we are not going to walk to town today; it's just too hot. We'll get a fresh start in the morning.

*Every day you can get a fresh start.*

## AUG. 27

We went to JC Penney's to shop for new school dresses. They had some really cute dresses, which we put on "Lay Away." When Mom's last summer paycheck comes, we'll go pay off the rest of the money and pick them up, just before school starts. We bought new school shoes and socks, too. Many of our old socks have holes in them.

[Historical note: Credit cards have not been invented yet, but some stores do give credit to trusted, valued customers. It is called "Putting it on your tab," I guess because every now and then they "tab"ulate how much you owe.]

## AUG. 28

We walked to town this morning, happily skipping most of the way, as we were on our way to buy school supplies at I T Bookstore, one of our favorite things to do. We bought yellow pencils with no teeth marks, nice clean erasers, a ream of notebook paper, spiral notebooks without snarled spirals, and, our favorite, a new box of crayons, the smell of which says "School!" like nothing else. Of course we wanted the largest box they had, each color so full of promise.   Now we are all set, and *really long* to get back to school.

**AUG. 29**

The twins have been shopping and packing for college. They are taking only their best clothes and shoes, leaving all of the ratty stuff behind. A clock radio from the shop, their graduation Smith Corona typewriters, new sheets and towels with iron-on GOTCH labels,  and their own iron and ironing board are all ready to go.

They'll be sharing a room in the brand new dorm called "Walker Hall," with dorm beds made to look like couches, couches with backs that are secret storage bins for the pillows and other important private things. We can hardly wait to see it all when we take them to Normal on Sunday.

At home, we younger girls are going to have the bedroom all to ourselves, and we'll each have our own bed for the first time ever. That will be so strange... and wonderful...maybe.

**AUG. 30**

Tonight we celebrated the end of another good year. Dad drove us home from town with us in the back of the Gotch Radio Specialties red delivery truck. Above the back window is written these words in flowing script: "There Goes Gotch". As we passed our house on the way to the Big House, we saw Mom on the front porch, so we all waved and yelled out together, "There

Goes Gotch!" Mom waved with a satisfied smile. "They may be Gotch's, " she thought, " but they're really *my* girls, and I'm proud of them all."

## AUG. 31

Today we took the twins to college, to their dorm room, with all their stuff, including the new matching spreads for their beds. Mom helped them set up the room. It looked so pretty. We were kind of putting off leaving, but then it really was time to go, so the twins walked us back down to the car. We were all smiling through our tears. We're going to miss them so much! We know things will never be the same again. Things will never be *quite* the same again.

# Final Thoughts

The Breakfast Nook/Kit. Table

Ginny & M.Alex. travelling

Twin Grads H.S.

*Hulda sets a nice table*

*Jeff*

*The Greenebergs*

**Big House Stairs**

*Mary Lew*

*Marie & Russ Ahearn*

*The Old Monk Painting at the Big House*

*Jerry, Johnny, Dorothy*

*Tillie, Millie, Pauline*

*S & L w/Kristy*

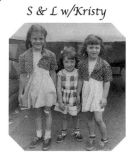

*Ruie Halpin*

No happy time that passes
is ever really gone

If it leaves a lovely memory
for looking back upon.
Robin St. John

# Appendix A  *Family History and Folklore*

## *Mom*

Mom, Hulda Emma Greenberg, (1/12/1908-10/3/1979) grew up in Bloomington, Illinois, sixty miles south of Streator, the daughter of German immigrants, Ernest and Emelie Pech Greeneberg.(Hulda spelled Greenberg without the middle "e". The German spelling was "Gruenberg".) Being the first in her family to go to college, Hulda attended Illinois State Normal University for two years, received a teaching degree, and accepted her first teaching position in Streator, a thriving community. She minored in drama in college and taught theatre classes, called "auditorium," her first year of teaching. Her experience acting in and directing plays at I. S. N.U. prepared her to direct the Washington Bi-Centennial Pageant performed at Marilla Park in Streator on July 4, 1932, an ambitious move for a twenty-four year old. The cast of two-hundred-fifty included Frank Gotch, whom she cast as the young George Washington. The rest of Hulda's thirty-two years of teaching she spent in the fourth grade. She was active in the Altar and Rosary Society at church, presided over the Parent Teacher's Association for years, and completed her Bachelor's Degree while she was teaching. Along the way, she raised four daughters and was a very involved grandmother to those who lived nearby. After retiring, she served as a volunteer at the hospital, and was involved in the leadership of AARP.

*Mom's Family*

Grandma Greeneberg, Emelie Pech Greeneberg, (2/24/1869 -1/15/1942). She was born in Preuben West Prussia Germany, immigrated to America in 1891. She married Ernest a few years later, March 14, 1895, at age 26; he was 19. She bore him six children. In 1900, they lived in Hopedale or Delavan, Illinois, (there are conflicting records) but by 1910, had moved to Bloomington. They attended the St. Luke's Evangelical and Reformed Church. Marcia remembers her well as a warm, loving woman who gave great hugs. She would sit down on a chair in the kitchen and envelop the twins, one in each arm. She loved to cook in her big kitchen, and was a great baker, baking all of her own bread for the week on Saturdays, and making homemade doughnuts that day as well. Her backyard was full of beautiful flowers, and a large fruit tree. They lived where Mom had grown up, on Olive Street in Bloomington. She died before Sharon and Linda were born.

Grandpa Greeneberg, Gustav Ernest W. Greeneberg, Jr, called "Ernest," (6/17/1876 - 4/23/1960) was a good, honest, rather silent man, a German immigrant who had been born in Russnau, Germany, and who had come to America with his family when he was seventeen. He was a boiler-maker for the Gulf, Mobile and Ohio Railroad, bringing his paycheck home each week, handing it over to his wife to manage the household, which she did with great frugality. After Grandma died, he married "Sugar bowl Luella". She went through all the money Grandma had saved, and had quite a temper. In one of her fits of rage she threw the sugar bowl at Grandpa, and thus procured her nickname for all time. She died shortly after of natural causes. He lived into his nineties, but never married again. When he was young, he smoked a pipe with cherry tobacco, but whenever we saw him, he was smoking a cigar. Grandpa was a Mason, a member of the Odd Fellows Lodge, and of the Order of the White Shrine of Jerusalem.

Great Grandparents: Gustav (Gus) Ernest Wm. Gruenberg, Sr. (1/19/1851 - 11/6/1921) and Rosalie (Rosa) Teschki Gruenberg (5/24/1849 - 8/6/1927) were both born in Stangendorf, West Prussia, Germany, but immigrated to the United States in 1893 with their eight children, Ann Elizabeth (Annie)(1873 - 1971), Hedwig Martha (Hattie)(1874 - 1948), Gustav Ernest Wm Jr. (Ernest) (1876 - 1960), Louise H. (Lizzie) (1879 - 1970), Emma Armanda, (1881 - 1970), Marie Martha (1885 - 1976), Minnie Augusta (1888 - ?)(), and Otto, (1890-1963). They left Bremen, Germany on December 9, arriving in Baltimore on the 28th with Elsa (Elsie) (1893 - 1918), the ninth, having been born during the voyage. Wow. They lived in Hopedale, IL. Gus and Rosa died there as well.

Other Great Grandparents: Friedrich (Fred) Wm. Pech (1831 -?) Westpreussen, Preussen, Germany married Caroline (Carrie) Heinz or Hinz (1834 -? ). They lived in West Prussia Germany, and had eleven children, our grandmother being number seven. In order of birth, they were: Josephine Grace (1851 - 1907), Augusta Pech Pehler (1858 - 1940), Florence (Flora)

Pech Pomrenke (1860 - 1917), Louise(a) Laverne (Lizzy) Pech Shoultz (1862 - 1948), Julius Adolf (1864 - 1941), Gustav Augustus (1866 -? ), Emilie Pech Greeneberg (1869 - 1942), Pauline Pech Pomrenke (1869 - 1942), Ernestine (Tine) Pech Bluhm (1874 - 1963), Carl Frederick (1876 - 1955), and Herman (1881 -? ).

Frieda Adolina Rosalie Greeneberg (8/23/1996 - 7/15/1902) Hulda's sister who died when she was only six years old. She died the same year Aunt Bee was born, when Martha was just two years old.

Aunt Martha, Martha H. Greeneberg Jacobssen (5/18/1899 - 12/7/1974) and Uncle Clarence, Clarence Karle Jacobssen (3/12/1895 - 7/1971) A quiet and gentle man whom we loved dearly, Clarence was part owner of the large and beautiful Beck Memorial Home in Bloomington, Illinois. Though they had no children of their own, Uncle Clarence *loved* children, serving on the board of the Baby Fold Orphanage for many years, where all of the children adored him. He also served on the board of Brokaw Hospital. Aunt Martha, Hulda's oldest sister, was the supportive wife, making it her business to know all of the right people in town by going to and giving lady's luncheons, teas and card parties. She also decorated fancy tables for weddings and other affairs. Whatever she was doing, she was sure to finish by four o'clock in the afternoon so that she could bathe, put on a fresh dress and make-up, and have a lovely dinner ready for Uncle Clarence's arrival home. At their home, we tasted elegance and civility beyond what we experienced at home. Aunt Martha's manner was rather stern, but she was very good to us, keeping us for a week or two, two girls at a time, every summer of our younger years. Because we stayed with them, they seemed to be our closest relatives.

Aunt Bee, Bertha A.Wall, (7/7/1902-) Hulda's older sister. A round, jolly person we rarely saw, and about whom we knew little, Bee lived in Bloomington all of her life, and was married to George A. Wall, (b.1898) whom we never knew. George worked for the city, but was killed as a young man when lightning struck a tree he was standing under; it fell on him resulting in his death. (No wonder Mom didn't want us to play under the oak tree during thunder storms.) Later on, she married a man named Warren Hassler. Aunt Bee was a good person with a heart of gold, and a good sense of humor. She was very different than our mother in her manner, but looked a great deal like Uncle Albert. She had four children close in age to the twins. Clarence (b.1924), Harry (b. 1926), Barbara Jean, (b. 1933), and Ronald W. (9/16/1938 - 7/9/2010). Harry had rather severe involuntary movements of his shoulder and facial muscles called "ticks". As children, we had no understanding of what might cause such a thing, so it was strange and a bit funny to us. Mom insisted that we be kind and compassionate about him. Clarence and Ronnie were both quite good looking, and did not have ticks. Barbara Jean was the daughter whom we never met but about whom we heard stories, for she was a real favorite with Aunt Martha. Mom rarely mentioned this family; they were our far-away relatives whom we knew the names of but not much else.

Uncle Leo, Leo Gustav Greeneberg (3/14/1906 -1963) and Aunt LaDonnah Maria Williams Greeneberg

( 11/13/1920-5/4/2004). Hulda's older brother and his
wife. They lived in Bloomington. They were both rather good looking and dressed nicely. He worked as a
state inspector for the Department of Agriculture, and
later for the city in maintenance. He also sang in a
barbershop quartet. They had two darling sons about
our age, Weldon (4/6/1943-9/12/2004 ) and Harlan (b.
7/8/1945), whom we met when we were teenagers and
wished they weren't our cousins. We pretty much only
saw these relatives at family funerals. "My how you've
grown since we've seen you," they would say. "It's been
a long time. You really shot up; you must be eating
your Wheaties!" Then it got quiet. Uncle Leo died
suddenly of a heart attack at just 56. While the twins
and Mom continued to have contact with them, Sharon
and Linda never saw them again.

Uncle Al, Albert Greeneberg (2/16/1912 - 6/21/1974)
Hulda's younger brother, a gentle, tolerant, lost soul
who had little education, who drank too much, who,
having never married, lived alone, who always looked
like he could use a good scrubbing, who worked at
times at the Canning Factory in Streator, but other
times was homeless and unemployed, whom we loved
but seldom saw, ended up in a mission in Bloomington, where he was saved by Jesus and turned his
life around, working for the mission, and becoming
a bright light. He loved his Bible! His hard life had
taken its toll, however, and he died of a stroke at age
sixty-two, after years of poor health.

*Dad*

Frank Robert Gotch, (3/19/1911-8/16/1965) the second

son of Slovakian immigrants, grew up in Streator IL.
Since they were rather wealthy, all of his clothes were
tailor-made. As a boy, Frank cleaned the spittoons in
his father's saloon, later, working as an usher at the
movie theatre, wearing the characteristic uniform and
pillbox hat. After attending Brown's Business College,
he went into business with his brothers, opening the
first Gotch Radio Specialties at 126 South Vermillion St. They later bought two buildings on Monroe
Street, the shop and the storage building on the alley.
He liked stiffly starched shirts and pinstriped suits,
usually wore bow ties and fedora hats, but he was
color-blind, so his wife would set out his clothes for the
day, to be sure they would match. He was professional
yet caring, cherishing every customer. He had four
sisters and two brothers who all thought they knew
better than he did about what needed to be done, how,
and why, even though *he* was the one who had gone to
Brown's Business College, and they hadn't. Pauline
and Jerry lived far away, so we hardly knew them.
The rest lived in our town, so we saw them often.
Frank's business was his life, but it was not the ideal
job for him. He was intelligent, sensitive, musical, and
maybe even a bit shy. Toward the end of his short
life, he became more and more silent and withdrawn.
He died at the age of fifty-four of stomach cancer that
spread throughout his body.

*Dad's Family*

Grandma Gotch, Mary (Mari Jurechko) Gotch,
(6/24/1879 - 10/25/1949) grew up in Kapusani, Slova-
kia, immigrating to America in 1891, at age twelve,
sponsored by her two older sisters. Streator had a

huge Slovakian community, including many of her relatives. She married John X. Gotch, Jr. on November 16, 1896 at St. Stevens Roman Catholic Church, bore him seven children, and probably lost a couple of others. She was a meticulous housekeeper, strictly adhering to her schedule: Wash on Monday, Iron on Tuesday, Mend on Wednesday, Market on Thursday, Clean on Friday, Bake on Saturday, and Rest of Sunday, and never missed mass, often dressed in a beautiful cloche hat. She was not a very social person, but was a very warm and loving grandmother, keeping lemon drops in her apron pocket for treats, and often serving up root beer floats, called "black cows." Loving flowers, she had the back yard full of them. She died of a heart attack at age seventy.

Grandpa Gotch, John Xavier Gotch, Jr. spelled "Goc" in the old country (Austria), where he was born, (10/29/1874 - 7/28/1930), Frank's father. He immigrated to America in 1887 at age twelve, and worked his way up to be the prosperous owner of the Budweiser Saloon on Main Street in Streator. A gregarious, fun-loving saloonkeeper, he would sometimes bring parties of people home from the saloon, cooking them dinner, entertaining them while Grandma went up to their bedroom, possibly because of her limited English vocabulary. Being an alderman in the city, and therefore aware of imminent raids, he continued to sell liquor during the Prohibition. The story we heard many times is that Grandpa Gotch, being a soft-hearted man, gave many loans and much credit to people during the depression, most of which were never repaid. The Budweiser Saloon sold the best chili in town, there were free pretzel sticks on the bar, and a large beer was five cents. We still have a good number of the beer glasses. They also sold many cigars from Cuba, and sponsored a baseball team, called the "Gotch's" John X., Jr was also a member of the first town band in Streator. He died at age fifty-six of stomach cancer, when Frank was only nineteen.

Aunt Millie, Ludmilla Gotch Balke, (9/16/1897 - 1/12/1988) Frank's oldest sister, grew up in Streator, IL attending St. Steven's school, where they taught in Slovak, at least in the early grades. After high school, she went to work in the office at Heenan's Department Store. She was hard working, loving, religious (Roman Catholic), and strongly opinionated. Most of her life she worked at the Gotch Radio selling records. When Grandma died, Millie became the Gotch matriarch. She was happily married to Joseph Peter (Jeff) Balke(3/19/1895 - 6/1/1971) but they had no children. Her one pregnancy, which happened to be the same year Linda was born, ended in a miscarriage (possibly a tubal pregnancy) in which she nearly died. This occurrence was never openly discussed. Jeff worked at Anthony Company, but his real gift, as far as we were concerned, was that he was a professional clown in the parades. He had a red nose, funny pants and shoes, and carried a plunger with a roll of toilet paper on it. What we didn't know back then is that he was the Santa Claus helper that came on Christmas Eve as well. They lived in a little house just a block from the railroad tracks, which had beautiful gardens all around the perimeter of the back yard. It was Aunt Millie, Uncle Jeff, their dog, Mickey, two chatty parakeets, and a little Bonsai tree on the table in the living room. She liked sweets, was generally overweight, and developed diabetes late in life. She had cataracts removed and wore "coke-bottle" glasses, so her eyes looked unusually large. It was the pattern of her life to be always learning something. Even as an old lady, she would be studying Russian or reading about classical music. She suffered for many years with arthritis, always hobbling around, but she never really complained, and didn't die until she was 91, of old age.

Aunt Pauline, Pauline Gotch Halpin (6/29/1899 - 1996?) Frank's second older sister, grew up in Streator, but married Steven Halpin, Sr. (1/30/1900 - 1/1987), a drummer with the Dick Jurgen's Orchestra in the Big Band Era. After traveling around with the band for a time, they settled down in Denver CO, and had a son, Steve Halpin, Jr, (4/26/1926 - 4/7/1996) who was called "Junior." He, too, became a professional drummer. While Junior was still a boy, Pauline divorced Halpin, and moved back to Streator for a while for the support of the family. During those years, Frank played a key role in helping to raise Junior. Eventually Pauline moved back to Denver, marring a man named George Pinson, a marriage that also ended in divorce. Later on, she married a third time to an avocado rancher in California, Harry Dawson, who subsequently died, so she moved back to Denver. Compared with the rest of the family, Aunt Pauline seemed very classy, with fancy hairdos and fancy clothes. She loved purple. Since she lived far away, we rarely saw her or even heard anything about her. Occasionally she sent us Christmas presents of things we had never heard of, like mukluk slippers, fresh grind salt and pepper shakers, and avocados.

Everyone seemed to laugh at such strange gifts. She died in her nineties. We hardly knew her, and we knew her husbands even less than we knew her. Steve Halpin, Jr.'s wife Ruie Allyn Halpin (10/8/24 - 10/29/90) became very close with Linda and Don in her later years.. She died of poly-cystic kidney disease, as did her sister, and her daughter, Kristine. Their son, Michael, was able to get a kidney transplant.

Aunt Tillie, Matilda Gotch Goldsmith, (2/15/1904 - 9/24/1983) Frank's third-oldest sister, grew up in Streator. With her sisters, she worked as a young woman at Heenan's Department store. Later, she worked at Thornton Floral Company. For as long as we knew her, though, she sold yard goods at JCPenney. She was the workhorse that kept the Big House clean and in good order. She was always cheerful, always chuckling about something, very loving, and could whistle like a canary or parakeet. She dated Uncle Ollie (Oliver) (8/21/04 - 6/5/1963) for years, but they didn't marry while his parents were alive because they were Christian Scientists and did not approve of him marrying a Catholic. When his parents had died, in 1946, they finally married, but by then they were too old to have children. They lived in a little upstairs apartment on Park Street, which they shared with his sister, Lucille, and a cat named "Gray Socks". They were only married ten years before Ollie was found in his armchair dead, apparently of a heart attack. Aunt Tillie had arthritis, and Alzheimer's late in life, dying at age 79. Her classic goodbye was, "Tootle-oo".

Uncle Johnny, John Xavier Gotch III, (3/18/1902 - 3/10/1973) Frank's older brother, and business partner. He lived alone in the Big House after Grandma died, and ate almost all of his meals at a little diner on North Vermillion Street. He always had Sunday dinners at Aunt Millie's, to which he brought a quart of ice cream. We know this, because if we ever visited Aunt Millie she would try to get us to eat up some of the ice cream. It always had ice crystals on it from being too old, and tasted horrible. Uncle Johnny was a whiz at electronics which he had learned when he was in the army, serving in World War II, where he was stationed on an island in the Pacific. He never was known to tell any stories about when he was in the war. As a young man, we know that he was something of an outdoorsman, for he went fishing in Canada every year. He never told stories about that, either. He was nearly always quiet and deadly serious. Like Millie, he loved classical music, and had it playing away in his little shop in the back of the store where he was the repairman for radios, phonographs, and televisions. If he got into a heated argument, as the Gotches were prone to do, he would often stutter when trying to make his point, sounding like a machine gun. Though he never married, we always heard the story of how he dated Mildred Halfpenny for twenty years or so, but at some point she had a grand mal seizure, which scared him, and the decision was made not to marry, perhaps in order not to pass on the epilepsy. He was a big encouragement to Sharon with regard to her love of mathematics. He died of Leukemia.

Uncle Jerry, Jerome Charles Gotch, (4/27/1914 - 7/30/1973) Frank's younger brother. He was one of Dad's business partners, but he lived very few years in Streator. While he was with us, he set up and ran the "Music in the Air" at Christmas, as well as taking many great photos of the family. He was a decorated flyer in the air force during World War II, and was also good with electronics. After the war, he worked on the DEW line up in Alaska, and did something for the government in Morocco, finally ending up in Florida. To us, growing up in Streator, these seemed romantic places to live! Besides that, he was married to Aunt Mary Lew, Mary Lew Burrows, (4/28/1931 - 10/20/1973) who was strikingly beautiful! Once they came to visit us with their daughter, Beth Ann, and we had a great time. Eventually, they were divorced, and Aunt Mary Lew married someone else, with whom she had a son, Shawn (b.1956 ). That marriage ended in divorce, and she remarried Uncle Jerry, who adopted Shawn. All of the local Gotches speculated that Shawn was actually Jerry's son to begin with, but there is no real reason to think that is true. Jerry and Frank looked the most alike of any in the family. Even their voices and mannerisms were similar.

Aunt Marie, Marie Grace Gotch Ahearn, (5/6/1916 -5/28/1994) and Uncle Russ, Edmond Russell Ahearn (7/9/1912 - 11/26/1976) Frank's little sister. A pleasant jovial person whose chuckle was quick to appear; she was still laughing at Uncle Russell's corny jokes at the end of her life. Early in her life, she was very sick with asthma. Barely making it through eighth grade, she was forced to quit, due to her poor health, and it was doubtful that she would live to adulthood since the asthma was so severe. Within a few years, though, medicine was discovered to control it, and she went on to marry and have three children, Judy (b.7/7/1942) and Billie (b.3/3/1945), with whom we shared every holiday, and Mary Jane (b.1/31/1959) who was born much later. Aunt Marie was a homemaker through and through, a marvelous seamstress, making her own and Judy's clothing. We remember her always in an apron, cooking hearty midwestern food. Rather short and round, she battled her weight, and was often on a diet of one sort or another. She was the family barber, which lead to much joking since Uncle Russ was nearly bald. In time, she suffered from arthritis, but loved to bowl, and was on a bowling team for many years. The last twenty years or so of Aunt Marie's life, Marcia lived near her, and they became very dear to each other. She died of a heart attack at age 78. Uncle Russell always had a few jokes to tell on any occasion, on any topic, jokes that were very corny. He was Irish and could do a pretty good Irish brogue. He had been a pitcher on a professional baseball team as a young man, and had been the coach of the little Hebron Green Giant basketball team the year they beat all of the other teams in the state of Illinois to win the state championship in 1952. All that was before he moved to Streator, where he was a teacher in the high school, and coached a few minor sports, but not basketball for some reason. He sold insurance, and died at sixty-four of pancreatic cancer.

*A Small Tribute to Our Sister*

Marilyn Lou Gotch Kennedy (9/20/1938 - 3/3/2001),

Marcia's twin sister, born five minutes after Marcia, she was Marcia's life-long companion and support person. Marilyn willingly took on the role of Mom's best helper, hard-working, responsible, wise, always willing to serve. We could rely on Marilyn; if she said she would do something, she would surely do it. Like a second mother, she cared for all of us sisters and our extended family as well. If anyone needed anything, she would find a way to make sure that we got it, being generous with her time, love, and resources. Marilyn received a bachelor's degree from I.S.N.U. , and a master's degree from Northern Illinois University. She was a middle school teacher of English literature and writing for thirty-two years in Hinsdale, IL. She married John (called Joe) Joseph Kennedy on December 30, 1961, and had two sons John Frank (b.March 9, 1963) and Patrick Gahen (b. June 30, 1964). Joe was an electrical engineer and executive at Motorola in Chicago, so they spent their weekdays in Hinsdale, and on the weekends they went to the farm that Joe had grown up on in Seneca IL to help with the farming. At the farm, Marilyn would clean and cook meals for the week for her in-laws, John and Helen Kennedy, another example of her servant's heart. Marilyn developed Guillain-Barre´ Syndrome, was paralyzed for many months and then died at age sixty-two. John F. married Jamie Kerestes from Streator, and they have one daughter, Hailey Nicole Kennedy (b. 1/20/2004). Joe, John F., & Patrick still run the award-winning farm in Seneca, IL. Patrick has not married.

# Appendix B   *Family Foods*

## *Holiday Foods*

### Aunt Marie's Chocolate Fudge

| | |
|---|---|
| 4 C. sugar | 2 pkg. choc. chips |
| 1 large can condensed milk | 1 tsp. vanilla |
| 1 stick butter | 1 C. chopped |
| | walnuts |

1 pt. jar of marshmallow fluff or crème

Combine sugar, milk and butter in a large pan and cook, stirring constantly, to soft ball stage. (When a bit is put into cold water it forms a little soft ball.) Remove from heat and stir in the chocolate chips, vanilla, nuts and marshmallow. Pour into a buttered 15 x 9 x 2 glass casserole. Let cool.

### Aunt Marie's Heavenly Fruit Salad

1 small Philadelphia cr. cheese (3 oz)
1/2 pint whipped cream, whipped
1 Tbs. mayonnaise
1 tsp. sugar
2 cans Royal Anne cherries, drained or bing cherries
1 can pineapple tidbits, drained
1 can mandarin oranges, drained
1/3-1/2 C. chopped pecans
2 C. miniature marshmallows

Make the day before; refrigerate overnight.
Mash the cream cheese until it is soft. Add the whip cream and sugar; whip until it is nice and fluffy. Mix in the mayo. Mix in the fruit, marshmallows and nuts.

# Christmas Eve Wild Mushroom and Sauerkraut Soup

1 onion, chopped
3 Tbs. butter
3 Tbs. flour
4 small cans sauerkraut juice
8 small cans water
1/2 lb. sliced dry wild mushrooms
Salt and pepper to taste
Sliced carrots, optional

Brown the onion in the butter and add flour, whisking continually. Slowly add the sauerkraut juice and water. Keep stirring. Add the mushrooms. Let simmer until mushrooms are well hydrated. Add carrots if you like, and season with S & P.  Serve in a beautiful soup tureen.

# Cookie Press Christmas Cookies
### (Recipe from Hulda's Aunt Marie)

2 sticks butter (1/2 lb.)
2/3 C. sugar
2 1/2 C. (scant) flour
1 egg, beaten
1 tsp. vanilla

Cream butter and sugar together. Add beaten egg and vanilla. Gradually add flour. Chill. Put through cookie press onto ungreased cookie sheet. Make sure cookie sheet is room temp. or the cookies will not stick to it. Bake 5-10 min. at 350°.

## Holiday Scalloped Corn

1 1/2 small envelopes of Saltine crackers
Milk and butter
2 cans cream style corn

Butter an oval baking dish. Preheat oven to 320°.
3/4 small envelope of Saltines, crushed per layer. Layer crackers, milk and butter clumps, 1 can of cream style corn. Repeat. Sprinkle with paprika.

Bake for 1 hr. or until golden brown.

## Holiday Three Vegetable Casserole

1 head of cauliflower, cut into florets
4-5 carrots, sliced into matchsticks
1 can Del Monte green beans
1 stick of butter, plain bread crumbs

Steam the cauliflower and carrots. Heat the beans.
Place in a large bowl (like the large yellow Pyrex),
keeping them separate as much as possible.
Top with the buttered breadcrumbs and serve.

**Rushka**      Makes 5 rolls    (Slovak: rozak)
Dough:
1 C. plain mashed potatoes
1 C. warm (not hot!) potato water, dissolve 1 1/2 pkg.
yeast in this)
2 sticks margarine melted into
1 C. warm milk
(Linda cut this to 1 stick, and it works)
2 eggs, well beaten
6+ C. flour (one of these may be whole wheat)
1/2 C. sugar
1/4 tsp. salt
Mix first 5 ingredients in a large bowl, making sure
nothing is too hot to kill the yeast. Combine dry ingredients, and add them a cup at a time to the wet ingredients. Knead until smooth and elastic, removing any
lumps of potatoes as they rise to the surface. Oil the
ball of dough, and place in an oiled container. Cover.
Refrigerate at least several hours. Original recipe says
overnight, which works best. It will fill the container. Take out. Knead on a floured board. Make into 5
equal balls. Cover and let rise for half an hour or so.
Roll or gently pat each ball into a rectangle, fairly
thin. Spread on filling to within one inch of the edge.
Roll up lengthwise. Grease with margarine or oil.
Place in greased oblong pans, cover with a dishtowel,
letting the early ones rise while you do the others. You
will have two in one pan and three in the other. Bake
at 350° for 45 – 50 minutes. Remove from the pans
immediately. Brush with margarine when you have
them out, and cover with old flour sack dishtowels to
cool. When cool, wrap in plastic wrap and foil. Freezes
pretty well, if wrapped well.

## Rushka Filling

Walnut:
Grind 2 pounds English Walnuts (food processor
works well)
Mix with 1 1/2 sticks margarine and sugar to taste
(abt. 1/2 C.)
Add milk to make it spreading consistency

Apricot:
1 container of dried apricots, chopped to pea size
water

Simmer this in a small pan until it is nice and mushy.
You may have to add water now and again. Mash with
a hand potato masher. Add a little sugar if you like.
Usually it doesn't need it.    Cool before spreading on
the dough.

Poppy seed:

1/2 pound poppy seed – ground
1/4 C. melted Crisco
1/2 C. sugar
1/2 C. hot water
1/4 C. applesauce (optional)

Where do you find 1/2 pound poppy seed? I never did.
You can buy Solo poppy seed filling in some grocery
stores. This may be an acquired taste. Of the choices
of rushka, this one was always the last to be eaten up.

## Holiday Sweet Potatoes or Yams

Cook yams with the jackets on (a large pan full) Peel
and mash, adding lots of butter, salt and pepper, and
a bit of brown sugar (optional)
  Put a spoonful of potatoes in a greased 8 x 12 casserole. Top with a marshmallow, and then cover the
marshmallow with more sweet potatoes to make a
little mound, continue so that you have about 4 across
and 6 down. Place 3 perfect pecans on each mound
evenly spaced to make a star.

Bake in a 350° oven for 30 minutes or so.


## Everyday Foods


## Aunt Martha's Chicken Salad   (for a lady's luncheon)

Combine the following ingredients with mayonnaise

    Cold cooked chicken breast
    Green grapes
    Pineapple tidbits
    Sliced almonds
    Sliced black olives
    Celery, bite-sized

# Aunt Martha's Ham Loaf and Special sauce

1 pt. whipping cream,whipped stiff
1 # ground lean pork
1 Tbs.. vinegar
1 # ground lean smoked ham
a bit of horseradish
1 C. breadcrumbs
3 eggs

Mix thoroughly. Place in pan and mark to cut into squares or make into a loaf. Bake at 300° for 1.5 hours.

Mix together and serve w/loaf

1 C. tomato sauce
1 C. milk or half and half cream
a bit of Worcestershire sauce

# Aunt Martha's Jell-O Salad

Bottom layer:
1 small pkg. lime or lemon gelatin,
mixed according to directions
a little salt
2 Tbs. vinegar
a good cup full of celery cut into tiny pieces
1 small can crushed pineapple, drained
1 med. cucumber chopped
Mix together and put in refrigerator to jell.

Top layer:
1 small pkg. lime or lemon gelatin, mixed
  according to directions
1 C. mayonnaise
2 – 8 oz. pkgs. Philadelphia Cream cheese
1 med. green pepper chopped and a little onion
juice
Cream the mayo and cream cheese together
and mix together with the other ingredients. Pour over
jelled bottom layer. Jell and serve.


## Aunt Martha's Slim Chicken Tetrazzini

3 C. cooked breast of chicken or leftover turkey
  in 2 in. pieces
6 oz. broad egg noodles – cook to tender

Sauce: Combine the following with 2 C. cold
water in saucepan. On medium, heat until bubbling
and thick.
  2 Tbs. dry milk
  1 1/2 Tbs. cornstarch
  2 tsp. instant chicken broth
  1/4 tsp. pepper
  1 tsp. salt
  1/2 tsp. onion powder
  Pinch of nutmeg
Combine with meat and noodles. Bake in
greased 9 x 13 pan for a while... half an hour or so at
350°.

## Betty Spirduso's Calico Bean Salad

1 can cut green beans, drained
1 can cut wax beans, drained
1 can kidney beans, drained
1/2 C. chopped green pepper (opt.)
A few onion slices (opt.)
3/4 C. sugar
2/3 C. vinegar
1/3 C. oil
1 tsp. salt
1 tsp. pepper

Mix sugar, vinegar, oil, S & P. Pour over the beans. Toss and refrigerate overnight. Will keep for a week in the fridge.

## Butterbean Soup

Cover a package of dry lima beans with water in a large bowl. (We grew up with the larger ones, but the smaller ones are just as good and cook faster.)

Soak for a couple of hours while you do something else or let them soak overnight. Add more water if you need to in order to keep them covered. Drain. Add beans to soup pot with new water to cover. Simmer for hours on the back of the stove until the beans are very soft. Check now and then to make sure they are covered with water. Mash a bit at the end with a potato masher. Add salt at the very end, to taste. To each bowl of butterbeans add a little pat of butter. Serve with salad and bread or crackers.

## Cornmeal Mush

Boil salted water and pour cornmeal in slowly while stirring with a whisk in the proportion of 3 C. water to each cup of cornmeal. Fill up platefuls and make a well in the middle. Pour in browned butter. Pour leftovers in greased loaf pan, cover, and refrigerate. Next day, fry slices and eat with syrup.

## Creamed chipped beef on toast

Make a white sauce, 2 Tbs. flour and 2 Tbs. butter for each cup of milk.

Melt the butter, whisk in the flour. Let cook for a bit, and then gradually whisk in the milk. Open a jar of dried beef and rinse it under the faucet. It is very salty.   Chop it up and add it to the white sauce. Serve over toast with a green salad on the side.

## Creamed Tuna on toast

Make a white sauce as in chipped beef recipe. Instead of beef, add 1 can of tuna and some peas.  Serve on toast.

## Cucumbers in Vinegar

This is a summer treat when these come fresh out of the garden.

Cucumbers, onions, red and green
peppers, and tomatoes (any/all)
1/2 C. white cider vinegar
1/2 C. cold water
2 Tbs. sugar
Salt & pepper

Make up the marinade, and pour over the vegetables. Let them marinate for a day or two in the fridge in a glass-covered container. Will keep for at least a week.

## Fried Smelt
There's nothing better than fresh fried smelt!

Rinse in water, cleaning out any remaining innards. Dip in beaten egg, and then cornmeal. Fry in oil or Crisco. Drain on paper towels. Serve with ketchup, homemade baked fries, and coleslaw or kidney bean salad.

## German Potato Pancakes

> 6 good-sized potatoes, peeled and grated
> 1 heaping Tbs. flour
> 1 egg

Combine and stir.   Meanwhile, have an iron skillet well greased and hot to start. When ready to fry, turn to medium.  Put a heaping spoonful in the pan, and spread out as for regular pancakes. Let it get golden brown and then turn over to brown the other side. Serve with applesauce or grape jelly.

## Grandma Greeneberg's Buffalo Fish
(The exact wording of the original recipe)

> Water to cover large white fish
> Salt
> 1-2 onions
> 1 big lump of butter

round spices   (pickling?)
leaves (bay)

Bring above ingredients to a boil in a roasting pan.
Add the fish and let cook 5-10 minutes. Put fish on
platter & keep warm. Add flour and milk to broth for
gravy. Cut fins off.

## Grandma Greeneberg's
## Hot German Potato Salad

1/2 C. roast, chicken, or bacon drippings
6-8 med. potatoes, cooked, peeled, & sliced
Enough flour to make a thick paste
2 C. water
1 slightly beaten egg
1 C. sugar
1/2 C. white vinegar
1/2 tsp. prepared mustard
Salt & pepper

Heat drippings in a skillet, and then remove from the
heat. Add the flour and stir to make a thick paste.
Add the water, stirring until well mixed. Place back
on low heat, stirring all the time, until it thickens.
Remove from the heat and add the egg, sugar, vinegar,
mustard, and a little S & P. Place back on low heat.
Stir. Cook for a bit.

Cook the potatoes with the jackets on, peel and slice.
Add some celery and chopped onion if you like.   Pour
the dressing over the potatoes.   Tastes even better the
second day.      Good luck.  Hulda E. Gotch

## Halushki Kapushki
(Slovak spelling – halusky kapustu)

    1/2 head of cabbage
    Butter
    Two or three large handfuls of flat egg noodles

Cut the cabbage in fine shreds. Sauté this in butter.
Meanwhile, boil the noodles in salted water until
tender.
Drain the noodles and add to the skillet with the cabbage.
Cook together for a bit, adding salt or butter to taste.

May be topped with grated cheese, but we never had it
that way.

## Hulda's Famous Baked Beans

    1 large can Van Camp's Pork and Beans
    1/4 C. Brown Sugar
    1/2 C. dark corn syrup
    1/2 C. ketchup
    1/2 onion, grated
    Bacon on top

Bake in large yellow Pyrex mixing bowl. (a double
recipe)

Bake in a slow oven for more than an hour, and then
let it sit and gel in the oven for an hour or two after.

# Hulda's Harvard Beets

Trim off the tops and roots of a pan full of beets. Boil in water until tender. Slip off skins and slice or dice.

Sauce: 2 Tbs. butter
     3 Tbs. sugar
     4 Tbs. vinegar
     1 tsp. cornstarch
     4 Tbs. lemon juice
     1/4 tsp. salt
     A sprinkle of pepper
Combine over med. heat, and stir until thickened. Pour over cooked beets. Store in refrigerator.

# Hulda's Homemade Egg Noodles

2 well-beaten eggs
All the flour they will take
1 tsp. salt

Beat the eggs, add the flour and salt. Roll a little thinner than piecrust on a floured board, and hang to dry on a drying rack or even the handle of the oven. When dry, cut into long strips, about 2" wide, and then cut those across into narrow strips. To cook, boil these noodles in salt water as usual, or cook right in the chicken broth. They are tasty with chicken and a bit of broth.

## Hulda's Special Chop Suey

1 lb. leg of veal, cubed
1 lb. pork shoulder, cubed
1 tsp. salt
2 Tbs. molasses
1 C. sliced onion
1 stalk celery cut up
1 small can mushrooms (or a few fresh)

Brown the meat in butter. Add next four ingredients
and sauté for 20 minutes. Sprinkle with flour and add
1 1/2 C. water. Bring to a boil. Reduce heat and add
the mushrooms. Pour sauce over chow mien noodles
and serve with sticky rice.

## Hulda's Sunday Roast   This smells heavenly
when you get home from church.
Pork and Beef Roasts were often baked together to
combine the flavors.

Coat the surface of the roast with salt & pepper.
Brown all sides in a skillet. Make slits in the top of
the meat with a sharp knife. Insert garlic buds. With
toothpicks, attach large sections of onion or halves
of small onions. Sprinkle pork roast with rosemary.
Arrange cut up carrots and potatoes around the edges.
Add some water to keep things moist. Bake for several
hours in a slow oven (325°). Meat should be well done.
Remove all to platter and keep warm while you make
the gravy.

To make the gravy, in a jar, shake a cup or so of water with 2 heaping Tbs. flour. Add to any drippings and liquid in the pan, and whisk over the heat until the gravy forms.

## Hulda's Swiss Steak

Round steak (top or bottom, a full slab)
Flour to flour the meat
1 C. chopped celery
1 C. chopped onion
1 C. chopped green or red pepper
1 can of tomato soup, diluted
Salt and pepper

Cut off all visible fat from the meat. Place on a cutting board and spread a layer of flour over the surface of the meat. Pound this into the meat with a large knife, on both sides, crisscrossing the knife. Brown this in a skillet with Crisco or oil. Place in a roasting pan. Top with the vegetables, salt and pepper, and the soup. Bake at 325° for a couple of hours, until the meat is very tender. Serve this with baked potato, putting the gravy on the potato as well as the meat.

## Johnny Mazetti
1 # ground beef
2 ribs of celery chopped
1 chopped onion
1 can of diced tomatoes or tomato sauce
1 C. dry elbow macaroni

Fry the hamburger, breaking it up, until it's brown.

Drain. Put back in skillet, and add the onion and celery. Cook for a bit, and then add the tomatoes or sauce. Let simmer for a bit. Meanwhile, boil the elbow macaroni in salted water until el dente. Drain, and add to the skillet with the other ingredients. Serve with grated Parmesan or Romano cheese.

## Kidney Bean Salad

Combine a can of kidney beans, drained, with a couple of tablespoons of pickle relish, some chopped celery, and a dollop of mayonnaise.

## Lentil Soup

Cover one package of raw lentils with water in a large bowl and soak until they fill the bowl. Drain and rinse. Add to soup pot with new water to cover. Add 1 Tbs. garlic powder and 1 Tbs. onion powder. Let simmer until the lentils are mushy. Add more water to keep lentils covered. 2 hours or so should do it. May mash a little bit at the end with a potato masher. Salt to taste. Add the salt last, for, if added earlier, it keeps the beans from getting soft.

## Linda's Birthday Spareribs

Country spare ribs (pork)
A1 sauce and ketchup in equal amounts.

Remove any excess fat from the ribs and brown them in a skillet. Place in roasting pan with sauce on top. Bake for several hours in a slow oven (325°), until the meat is falling off the bone. Serve with baked potato and baby lima beans.

## Luckshaw

Cook potatoes with the jackets on, a pan full. Peel, mash, and add salt (or use left over mashed pota- toes). Preheat oven to 350°. Add enough flour to hold together (add gradually until you think you can roll it out). Flour the board and roll out dough like pie crust. Bake on an ungreased cookie sheet until golden brown. Flip over and brown the other side. Remove from oven and brush with melted butter. Stack them up with a plate on top (covered) until all are baked, keeping them warm on the top of the stove. Cut the stack like a cake into pie shaped wedges. To eat, roll up each section, and eat one at a time. Serve with celery and carrot sticks.

## Machunka Gravy

Make gravy from the drippings from a beef roast as usual, except add a can of sauerkraut juice for the liq- uid. Pour over toast or bread. We had this for dinner sometimes, and loved it.

## Porcupine Balls

> 1# ground beef
> 1 can tomato soup
> 1/2 an onion, chopped or some dry onion flakes
> 1/2 C. uncooked white rice

1 egg
a dash of Worcestershire sauce
Salt and pepper
Mix all together. Make into walnut-size balls. Dilute
tomato soup with a can of water and put meat and
soup in a covered casserole. Bake at 350° for an hour
or so. Serve with cooked carrots and cabbage, and
bread to soak up the tasty sauce.

## Potato Soup

6 med. potatoes
2 celery stalks, with the tops in large chunks
1 small onion, peeled, cut up in large chunks
4 or 5 slices of bacon
Milk (optional)

Boil potatoes, celery and onion together in water.
Strain, saving the liquid. Remove the onion and celery
and throw away. Mash the potatoes, leaving it a bit
lumpy. Meanwhile, cut up the bacon and fry to crisp.
Remove from pan. Add liquid and flour to drippings,
making a roux. Once it thickens, thin with reserved
liquid (add milk if you like), making it into soup, adding the potatoes and bacon.

## Tuna casserole

Make a white sauce as in chipped beef recipe. (Or use
a can of mushroom soup.) Add a few sautéed mushrooms, and a can of tuna. Meanwhile, be boiling a
couple of cups of dry egg noodles in salted water.
Once they are soft, drain the noodles and mix in with
the sauce. Pour into greased casserole and top with

crushed potato chips. Bake until bubbly, half an hour
or so, at 350°.

## Vegetable Beef Soup (or leave the beef out)

In a pot of water, put the following:

> Cut up cooked beef chunks, leftover roast
> 1 onion, chopped to bite-size
> 2-3 stalks of celery, bite-size
> 2-3 carrots, bite-size
> 1 C. or so of corn
> 1 C. or so of beans
> 1 C. or so of peas
> 1 can of cut up tomatoes (or fresh)
> minced parsley, fresh or dry
> a small sprinkle of basil and marjoram

Simmer together for an hour or more, until vegetables
are cooked and flavors are developed. Near the end,
add some flat egg noodles.

## *Desserts*

## George's Caramel Apples

> 1 can Eagle Brand milk
> 2 C. brown sugar
> 1 stick margarine
> 3/4 C. white corn syrup

apples
wooden popsicle sticks
chopped peanuts

Combine first four ingredients and bring to a boil in a heavy pan (not a double boiler). Stir, and let boil about 15 minutes or to 350° on a candy thermometer. Insert a stick in each apple, and dip apples quickly into the caramel. Plunge immediately into ice water and place on wax paper to dry. Roll in chopped peanuts.

## Grandma Gotch's (Mary Gotch) Oatmeal Cookies

1 C. sugar
1 C. shortening
2 C. oatmeal
1 C. raisins
1 heaping tsp. cinnamon
1 scant tsp. baking soda in 4 Tbs. milk
2 eggs
2 C. flour
A pinch of salt
1 tsp. vanilla

Just mix all together and spoon off onto cookie sheet. Bake at 400°, 8-10 min.

## Hulda's Strawberry Angel Food Cake

1 round angel food cake
1 package of strawberry gelatin
1 qt. fresh strawberries, cut up
  save a few halved for garnish
1 pt. whipped cream, whipped  (Cool whip can
  be used, but it is not as good.)

First, make up the gelatin according to directions on the box, and let it be jelling.
Using a fork and/or fingers, ½ inch below the top, in the center of the cake, dig out small pieces of the cake to within 1" of the outside and bottom. Place in bowl.
Cut up the strawberries and whip the cream.
Break up the gelatin into bite-sized pieces and combine with the cake pieces, cut up strawberries and half of the whipped cream. Stuff this back into the hole, making it even on the top. Frost the whole thing with the rest of the whipped cream and decorate with the halved strawberries. Store covered in the refrigerator.

## Ice Box Cookies (a Fall tradition)

| | |
|---|---|
| 1 C. brown sugar | 1 tsp. baking soda |
| 1 C. white sugar | 1 tsp. cinnamon |
| 1 ½ C. butter | 1 tsp. mace |
| 3 eggs | 1 C. chopped walnuts |
| 4 C. flour | |

Mix together, then shape into logs. Wrap the logs in wax paper, twisting the ends, and place in refrigerator up to a week, or in the freezer for longer storage. When they are hard, remove and slice thinly with a sharp knife. (1/8 in. to 1/4 in. or so) The thinner they are, the crunchier they are.
Bake at 400° for 8-10 min. on ungreased cookie sheet.

## Oakland Park School Apple Crisp

4-5 C. apples, peeled or unpeeled,
    but cored and sliced
1 Tbs. lemon juice

Topping:
    1/3 C. flour
    1 C. uncooked old-fashioned oats
    1/2 C. brown sugar
    1 tsp. cinnamon
    1/2 C. chopped walnuts
    1/3 C. melted butter
Place apples in greased shallow casserole. Sprinkle with the lemon. Mix dry topping ingredients, add the melted butter, crumble up with your fingers and sprinkle over the apples.   Bake at 350° for 30 minutes.

# Pickles

## Hulda's Bread and Butter Pickles

1 gallon cucumbers – slice 1/2 " thick
4 large onions – slice
Let stand an hour in cold salt water

Solution:
    1 qt. vinegar
    2 C. sugar
    1 tsp. black pepper
    1 tsp. celery seed
    1 tsp. mustard seed

1 tsp. dry mustard
1 tsp. turmeric

Boil solution. Add cukes slowly and let boil until they are discolored. Put in hot jars and seal. They will be pickled in a couple of weeks.

## Hulda's Garlic Dill Pickles

Soak cukes overnight in cold water

Quarter cukes as desired for packing. Place 1 slice of onion and a garlic clove in the bottom of each canning jar. Pack cucumbers closely. Place a sprig of dill on top and pour over hot vinegar solution. Seal. They will be pickles in a couple of weeks.

Solution:   1 qt. cider vinegar
              1 qt. white vinegar
              1 qt. water
              1 C. salt
Boil 2-3 minutes.

# Appendix C *Indoor Games*

## Button, Button, Who has the Button

All sit in a circle. One person is "it". "It" closes her eyes and counts out loud to some specified number, as in Hide and Go Seek. A button is passed from hand to hand with hands behind the back. When the final number is reached, "It" has to guess who has the button, and which hand it is in. If s/he guesses right, that person becomes "It". If not, s/he counts again and the button continues being passed around.

## I Spy

All sit in a circle. One child sees something in the room, and gives clues about what it is, saying "I spy something that is..." (often a certain color) Others in the circle guess what it is. If they can't guess it, they can ask for more clues. The person who guesses it first can spy the next thing.

## Hide the Thimble

Someone hides a thimble somewhere in plain sight, but hard to see, while everyone else is out of the room. When they come back, they have to find the thimble. The one who hid it can give clues about whether they are close or far away, "cold" being far away, and "hot" being right on top of it. The one who finds the thimble first hides it the next time.

"What is a thimble?" you may ask. A thimble is a tool used in hand sewing. It is usually made of metal in the shape of a fingertip, and its purpose is to protect your middle finger as it pushes the needle through the material. Even the thread end of a needle is rather sharp, especially if you have to penetrate very thick material. Every girl in Hulda's era would have treasured her *own* thimble. Hulda's thimble is gold, with a flowery design and a monogrammed "G" for Greeneberg (and later Gotch). Linda has this thimble. It is quite small, as Hulda's fingers were very thin.

## School

Playing school is a game to be played on a nice big staircase. Everyone starts on the bottom step, and one "teacher", ideally the oldest and perhaps the smartest child, faces the class. The teacher gives each one, in turn, a question. If it is answered correctly, that child moves up one step (one grade). A missed question makes you stay on the same stair. The first one to the top either wins the game, or gets to be teacher the next time. Questions should be appropriate to the age of the child, but can be from many different areas of study, for example, spelling, geography, mathematics, science, etc.

## I'm Thinking of Something

Someone says, "I'm thinking of something..." and begins to give clues about what that something is. The others can ask questions that can be answered "yes" or "no". The one who guesses correctly may be the next one to think of something, or it can just be the next person to think of a good "something."

## "My Father Owns a Grocery Store"

First person says, "My father owns a grocery store, and in it he sells..."(something that begins with A.) say "Apples." The next person starts over with "My father owns a grocery store, and in it he sells, "Apples and Bananas" ( a product beginning with 'B') On it goes until you get to the father who sells Apples to Zucchini. Each person has to remember all of the products in order to win. If you forget one, you are out, and play continues.

## Telephone or Gossip

Everyone sits in a circle. The first person whispers something to the one next to them and the message is passed on to the next until the last person, who says the message out loud. Often the last sentence is totally different, and can be quite funny.

## Clapping games

This was definitely a girl's only game.... never saw a boy do this. There are countless versions of this kind of game. The most familiar one to us went like so:

*Peas porridge hot, Peas porridge cold,*
*Peas porridge in the pot, Nine days old.*
*Some like it hot, Some like it cold,*
*Some like it in the pot, Nine days old.*

Motions: two girls facing each other fairly close together       Peas - both hands to lap    Porridge - clap Hot - right hand to right hand   Peas - lap   Porridge - clap   Cold - left hand to left hand   Peas - lap   Porridge - clap   In the - R to R   Pot - clap   Nine- L to L - Days - clap -  Old - L to R and R to L, etc. See how fast you can eventually go.

## Incredibly Boring Songs to sing in the car:

*A Hundred Bottles of Beer on the Wall*

*A hundred bottles of beer on the wall,*
*a hundred bottles of beer,*
*What would happen if one should fall?*
*Ninety-nine bottles of beer on the wall.*
*Ninety-nine bottles of beer on the wall,*
*ninety-nine bottles of beer.*
*What would happen if one should fall?*
*Ninety-eight bottles of beer on the wall.... Etc.*

*Found a Peanut*

*Found a peanut, found a peanut,*
*found a peanut just now.*
*Just now I found a peanut,*
*found a peanut just now.*
*Cracked it open, cracked it open,*
*cracked it open just now.*
*Just now I cracked it open, cracked it open just now.*
    *It was rotten, ...*
    *Ate it anyway...*
    *Got a tummy ache...*
    *To the doctor...*
    *Operation...*
    *Died anyway...*
    *Went to heaven...*
    *Found a peanut... ad nauseum*

*The Ants Came Marching*

*The ants came marching two by two, Hurrah, Hurrah*

*The ants came marching two by two, Hurrah, Hurrah*
*The ants came marching two by two,*
*The little one stopped to (make this up; it has to rhyme*
*with "two", and then "three, etc.)*
  *Example: tie his shoe or say "achoo"*
*And they all kept marching down, and around,*
*on the ground, Boom, Boom, Boom*

(Continue on, three by three, then four by four, etc.

## A couple of games
### for keeping little hands busy

  Interlock fingers with the fingers down or in.
Fold hands so that the thumbs come together.
"Here is the church."
Extend the two index fingers up.
"And here is the steeple."
Rotate the hands out, opening the thumbs (doors),
exposing all of the fingers.
"Open the doors, and see all the people."

  One person places a flat hand on a flat surface, say a
lap. The other person places a hand on top of it. First
person then places a second hand on top of that, and
the second person places the last hand, then the bottom hand is removed and placed on top, over and over,
slowly speeding up until chaos ensues.

# Appendix D    *Outdoor Games*

Many outdoor games have a person called "it." There are many ways to decide who is "it." One is to form a ring with everyone extending their fists into the middle. Then someone taps each fist while saying a rhyme.

Here is a popular rhyme:

One potato, two potato, three potato,
FOUR
Five potato, six potato, seven potato, MORE......
the "more" fist goes behind your back and the rhyme goes again until only one person or fist is left. That person is "it".

Another rhyme:

Eenie, Meenie, Minie, Moe
Catch a tiger by the toe,
If he hollers, let him go
Eenie, Meenie, Minie, Moe    The last
"Moe" fist goes behind your back, then go again, and again and again until only one is left. That person is "it." These methods can also be used to determine who goes first.

When a game is decided upon, it may be that no one wants to be "it". One after another may yell out "not it", "not it", "not it" until the last person to say "not it" is "it."

## Tag

This is the easiest outdoor game because it takes no equipment, just lots of energy. "It" chases the other(s), even two people can play, until s/he tags the other, then that person is "it" and the chase goes on.

Problems occur when there is a dispute as to whether the person was tagged or not.

## Hopscotch

A grid is drawn on the sidewalk with chalk. Our grids only went to 8, with 1,2,&3 in a straight row, then 4 & 5 next to each other, 6 in the middle, and then 7 & 8 next to each other. Everyone has a stone or piece of broken glass for a marker, and you all toss your marker into the first square to begin. Any square with a marker in it has to be hopped/jumped over. You hop to the top, turn around and hop back, landing with two feet on 4 & 5 and 7 & 8 if they are not occupied, picking up your piece on the way back. Then you throw your piece to the next square, and go again until you miss by stepping on a line or falling or throwing your piece so that it doesn't land in the right place. The first person to go all the way to 8 and back is the winner. It gets pretty tricky when you have to jump over several spaces in a row and land on only one foot.

## Hide and Seek

Few people have not played hide and seek in their lifetime. It can be played equally well inside or out. Someone who is "it' covers their eyes and counts to 100 or other designated number depending on the age of the players and how big the area of play is. While "it" is counting, the others hide. "Ready or not, here I come," says "it" when the counting is over and s/he goes off to find the hidden players. In the outdoor version, if "it" sees you, you have to race to "home" (we used the oak tree). If you touch first you are home free, but if "it" touches first, you are now "it". When the last person just cannot be found and everyone is tired of the game, "it" may yell out "Ollie, Ollie Oxen all in Free" to let that person know the game is over.

## Kick the Can

This is a game we play frequently in the summer in the alley. A old empty can is placed in the middle of a circle drawn in the dirt. Everyone playing is just outside of the circle. Someone runs in and kicks the can, the harder the better, and all of the kids scatter to hide. When "it" has the can replaced in the center of the circle, s/he yells, "Freeze!" Players have to immediately stop moving. "It" looks to see if any are visible, calling out their names. These kids become the prisoners. As "it" goes to look for more players, someone may run in and kick the can again releasing all of the prisoners. A hiding player may also run into the circle and yell out "Ollie Ollie Oxen, All in free!" at which time everyone runs to get in the circle and the last one in has to be "it."

## Mother May I?

One person is designated the mother, and all the rest of the players line up pretty far away. Mother gives to one player after another some instruction, for instance, "Janey, go three baby steps, " or "Tom, go one giant step." If the player responds with "Mother may I?" and if Mother says "yes" they may go. If Janey or Tom just go without asking, they have to go back. For fun, Mother may respond with "no" just as well. In addition to giant steps and baby steps, there are hops, skips, and scissors steps. The person who first gets all the way to Mother wins and gets to be the next Mother.

## Statues
One person holds the hand of another twirling around and flinging them out, letting go. That person has to freeze in the position that they land in. It makes for a strange looking yard full of statues in the end.

## Jump Rope
Nearly every girl has her own jump rope made from a piece of woven clothesline. To measure for the right length, step on the rope and stretch it up to your hands with your arms bent. Leave a little extra for tying a knot in each end so it doesn't slip out of your hand. With this rope you can jump to your heart's content, fast or slow, in place or going down the street. It is fun to count and see how many times you can jump without missing.

   Group jumping is fun, too, but it takes at least three girls, two to twirl the rope, and one to jump...or two can jump at one time. The twirlers begin twirling the rope and the girl jumping must jump in just at the right time to keep the rope turning. This is usually done to a song or rhyme which helps keep the rhythm. Here are a few of the silly songs.

> *Down by the river where the green grass grows,*
> *there sat Linda, pretty as a rose.*
> *Along came Joe and kissed her on the cheek.*
> *How many kisses did she get this week?*
> *One, two, three, four,....*

At the last line, the twirling gets faster, and sometimes even faster, called "red pepper." The girl jumping keeps going until she misses and it is someone else's turn.

Here is another rhyme:　*Cinderella, Cinderella*
*Went upstairs to kiss her fella*
*How many kisses did she get?*
*One, two, three, etc.*
Sometimes the rhyme tells you to do certain tricks
while you are jumping. For instance,
*Teddy bear, Teddy bear, turn around;*
*Teddy bear, Teddy bear, touch the ground.*
*Teddy bear, Teddy bear, shine your shoes,*
*Teddy bear, Teddy bear, read the news.*
*Teddy bear,Teddy bear, go upstairs,*
*Teddy bear, Teddy bear, say your prayers.*
*Teddy bear, Teddy bear, turn out the light,*
*Teddy bear, Teddy bear, spell "Goodnight."*
*G - O - O - D - N - I - G - H - T*　(then jump out
and it is the next person's turn.)
Some girls even can jump with the twirlers twirling
two separate ropes which go in opposite directions.
This takes a great deal of practice and coordination.

## Jacks

You need the small red ball, 10 or 12 jacks, and a nice
flat place to sit with a smooth floor, like on the porch
or sidewalk.

Every trick must be accomplished after throwing the
ball up and letting it bounce only once before you catch
it with your dominant hand.

Onesies - Toss the jacks onto the floor. Throw the ball
up, pick up one jack, put it in your left hand and catch
the ball with your right hand after it bounces once.
Proceed to pick up them all, one at a time. Moving any

of the jacks other than the one you are picking up, or if the ball bounces more than once, makes you lose your turn.

Twosies - pick up two at a time.

Threesies - Pick up three at a time. Continue on... Foursies, Fivesies, Sixies, Sevensies, Eightsies, Ninsies, Tensies, Elevensies, Twelvesies (all in one scoop). Tossing the jacks so that they separate a good distance for whatever number you are on is part of the strategy.

Further moves include:

"Under the fence "- instead of putting the jacks in your hand, you slide them, one at a time or two at a time, etc. under your left hand which is resting on its baby finger side before catching the ball.

"Pigs in the pen" - Cup the left hand down on the floor, and slide the jacks, one at time, two at a time, or whatever, into the little pen you have created, before you catch the ball.

There is another move that goes "Pick a cherry, eat a cherry, throw the pit away." Does anyone know how that goes? Write to us, and we will include it in the next edition. Feel free to write and tell us of other moves as well. There may be many others.

First one to go through all of the moves wins.

# Appendix E

## *Fun Personality Contrasts*

Hulda's Girls: Four very unique women. Can you guess who has which traits?

Fill in the blanks at the end.

1. If she were a season, what would she be?
 A) Summer  B) Winter  C) Spring  D) Fall

2. If she were a kind of music?
 A) Classical B) Jazz  C) Popular  D)  C&W or
 or Hymns                Nursery
                         Rhymes

3. If she were a hair color?
 A) Red  B) Blonde  C) Brown  D) Almost Black

4. If she were an element?
 A) Water  B) Wind  C) Earth  D) Fire

5. If she were a kind of food?
 A) Meat /Potatoes  B) Chocolate  C) Chicken soup
        & Pie          & Salad        & Apple Crisp
 D) Mac & Cheese & popcorn
6. If she were a color?
 A) Blue  B) Yellow  C) Green  D) Red/Purple

7. If she were a time of day?
 A) Morning  B) Night  C) Lazy  D) Evening
                       Afternoon    (Late
                                    Bloomer)

8. If she were a job to be done?
A) Paint  B) Chop wood   C) Scrub  D) Dust

9. If she were a game to be played?
A) Scrabble  B) Scattergories   C) Checkers
D)  Cards       or Sorry          or Monopoly

10. If she were a destination?
A) The ocean  B) The lake  C) The mtns. D) The
                                         farm

11. If she were a painter, who would she be?
A) Grandma B) Rembrandt C) Matisse D) Monet
Moses

12. If she were a musical instrument?
A) cello  B) viola  C) oboe  D) drum

13. If she were a book?
A) adventure   B) novel   C) children's   D) recipe

14. If she were a hat?
A) chef's hat B) colorful hat C) newsboy  D) straw sun
               w/ veil          hat          hat
15. If she were a bird?
A) canary/  B) hen   C) mourning dove  D) peacock/
meadowlark            in a cage         woodpecker

16. If she were a Peanuts comic strip character?
A) Lucy  B) Linus  C) Charlie Brown   D) Peppermint
                                         Patti
17. If she were a type of vehicle?
A) Chevy  B) Buick   C) Corvette  D) Volkswagen

18. If she were a punctuation mark?
    A) !  B) .  C) ;  D) ?

19. If she were a form of water?
    A) plain water  B) ice  C) boiling water  D) steam

20. If she were a form of fire?
    A) match/  B) candle  C) fireplace  D) fire in a
    wildfire                fire           cook stove

21. If she were a road?
    A) neighborhood street         B) Main St.
       C) blacktop country rd.   D) quiet lane

22. If she were a kind of sky/weather?
    A) stormy/   B) fair/   C) fog/rain D) fair/
    tornado      clearing              partly cloudy

23. If she were a vase of flowers?
    A) daisies/ glass vase B) white peonies/white ceramic

    C) red roses/ crystal vase  D) Gerbera daisies/ black
                                                    vase

24. If she were an animal?
    A) cat  B) lioness  C) friendly  D) dog
                           dragon

25. If she were a day?
    A) a vacation day              B) a work day
       C) a day at the circus      D) a travel day

26. If she were a day of the week?
    A) Saturday  B) Monday  C) Sunday  D) Wednesday

27. If she were a kind of pie?
    A) rhubarb  B) lemon   C) apple   D) impossible/
       custard      meringue                   no crust

28)  If she were a card game?
    A) War   B) Solitaire   C) Go Fish   D) Bridge

Fill in your guesses below by putting the correct letter next to each number. See how your answers compare with ours.

MARCIA

| 1 | 2 | 3 | 4 | 5 | 6 |
|---|---|---|---|---|---|
| 7 | 8 | 9 | 10 | 11 | 12 |
| 13 | 14 | 15 | 16 | 17 | 18 |
| 19 | 20 | 21 | 22 | 23 | 24 |
| 25 | 26 | 27 | 28 | | |

MARILYN

| 1 | 2 | 3 | 4 | 5 | 6 |
|---|---|---|---|---|---|
| 7 | 8 | 9 | 10 | 11 | 12 |
| 13 | 14 | 15 | 16 | 17 | 18 |
| 19 | 20 | 21 | 22 | 23 | 24 |
| 25 | 26 | 27 | 28 | | |

SHARON

| 1 | 2 | 3 | 4 | 5 | 6 |
|---|---|---|---|---|---|
| 7 | 8 | 9 | 10 | 11 | 12 |
| 13 | 14 | 15 | 16 | 17 | 18 |
| 19 | 20 | 21 | 22 | 23 | 24 |
| 25 | 26 | 27 | 28 | | |

LINDA

| 1 | 2 | 3 | 4 | 5 | 6 |
|---|---|---|---|---|---|
| 7 | 8 | 9 | 10 | 11 | 12 |
| 13 | 14 | 15 | 16 | 17 | 18 |
| 19 | 20 | 21 | 22 | 23 | 24 |
| 25 | 26 | 27 | 28 | | |

Our Answers

**Marcia**: 1-A, 2-D, 3-C, 4-B, 5-D, 6-A, 7-C, 8-D, 9-B, 10-B, 11-A, 12-B, 13-C, 14-D,15-C, 16-B, 17-A, 18-D, 19-D, 20-B, 21-C, 22-C, 23-A, 24-D, 25-A, 26-A, 27-D, 28-C

**Marilyn**: 1-B, 2-C, 3-D, 4-C, 5-A, 6-C, 7-B, 8-C, 9A, 10-D, 11-B, 12-A, 13-D, 14-A, 15-B, 16-C, 17-B, 18-B, 19-B, 20-D, 21-A, 22-D, 23-C, 24-B, 25-B, 26-D, 27-C, 28-D

**Sharon:** 1-C, 2-B, 3-A, 4-D, 5-B, 6-D, 7-A, 8-B, 9-C, 10-A, 11-C, 12-D, 13-A, 14-B, 15-D, 16-A, 17-C, 18-A, 19-C, 20-A, 21-B, 22-A, 23-D, 24-C, 25-C, 26-B, 27-B, 28-A

**Linda:** 1-D, 2-A, 3- B, 4-A, 5-C, 6-B, 7-D, 8-A, 9-D, 10-C, 11-D, 12-C, 13-B, 14-C,15-A, 16-D, 17-D, 18-C, 19-A, 20-C, 21-D, 22-B, 23-B, 24-A, 25-D, 26-C, 27-A, 28-B

How about you? What would you be in each category?

# Appendix F

## *Aunt Millie's Candy Tin*

SEPT.  Spice gumdrops, w/purple cloves

OCT.  Candy corn

NOV.  Chocolate covered peanuts

DEC.  Hard candy Christmas ribbons

JAN.  Snow caps –(white beads on chocolate) -Pareils

FEB.  Conversation hearts & red cherry jelly hearts

MARCH  Soft Spearmint Leaves

APRIL  Pink, white, and brown coconut bars

MAY  Brach's Bridge mix  - Yuk!

JUNE  Orange Circus Peanuts

JULY  Root beer barrels

AUG.  - Saltwater taffy from summer vacation

Other candies that showed up: lemon drops, boxed chocolates, M & M's, plain and peanut, Red hot cinnamon hearts, Kraft Caramels, Good 'N Plenty Licorice, and candy buttons on a long paper ribbon, caramel creams (bulls' eyes), and peanuts w/ a crunchy coating.

# About the Authors

**Sharon Gotch Cobb** and her husband Peter live on Cape Cod, Massachusetts. Their careers centered on teaching the gifted and talented, and both worked as consultants developing public school gifted and talented programs throughout the United States. Sharon and Peter chose not to have children of their own. Sharon has previously published books for the education market.

**Linda Gotch Helmich** and her husband Don live in the mountains of Colorado. They have two married sons, and six lively grandchildren. After transitioning from a career as a registered nurse, Linda became a professional watercolorist. Although she has had poetry published, this is her first book in print. She is the co-author, illustrator, and publisher.

**Marcia Gotch Micklos** and her husband Andrew live in Illinois near four of their five grown children. The quintessential "Grammy", she has fourteen grandchildren, and two great-grandchildren. Her other passion is volunteering at Illinois Cancer Care in Peoria, IL.

## QUICK ORDER FORM

If you enjoyed this book and would like to order additional copies for yourself or friends, please check with your local bookstore, favorite online bookseller, or the website *www.lindahelmich.com* and place your order.

OR: FAX order: 970-947-9206  Send this form.

OR:  Send this order form to Barnhouse Books,

4006 C.R. 115, Glenwood Springs CO 81601.

Please send the following books. I understand that I may return them for a full refund (less shipping) if dissatisfied for any reason.

Title:_____

# of books _____@ $16.95 each
                         Book Total _____

($1.46 per book)(CO only)   Tax _____

                         Shipping _____

                         Total _____

(Please print)

Name: _____

Address: _____
City: _____
State: _____       Zip code: _____
Phone #
              _____
Email address:

              _____

Shipping by air: U.S. $4.00 for first book and $2.00 for each additional book.  International: $9:00 for first book; $5.00 for each additional.

MAKE CHECKS TO :  Barnhouse Books